A History of Collectibles and Memorabilia

Fifty Years of
Stock Car Racing

A History of Collectibles and Memorabilia

Fifty Years of
Stock Car Racing

KEN BRESLAUER

PHOTOGRAPHY BY BRIAN CLEARY

DESIGN BY TOM MORGAN

DAVID BULL PUBLISHING

Photography of memorabilia and collectibles copyright 1998 by Brian Cleary. Photograph on page 8 by Dozier Mobley, and page 9 and back cover (Petty) by Don Hunter. All other photographs are from the collection of the Author.

We recognize that some words, model names, and designations mentioned in this book are the property of the trademark holder. We use them only for identification purposes. This is not an official publication.

First Printing.

Library of Congress Cataloging-in-Publication Data
    Breslauer, Ken, 1957–
    Fifty years of stock car racing: a history collectibles and memorabilia
    / by Ken Breslauer : photos by Brian Cleary.
    p. cm.
    Includes index.
    ISBN 0-9649722-5-5
    1. Stock car racing—Collectibles—United States—Pictorial works. 2. NASCAR (Association)—Collectibles—Pictorial works. 3. Stock car racing—United States—History. 4. NASCAR (Association)—History. I. Title.
    GV1029.9.S74B74 1997
    796.72'0973'075—dc21

Book and cover design:
Tom Morgan, Blue Design,
San Francisco, California.

Printed in Hong Kong.

David Bull Publishing
4250 East Camelback Road
Suite K150
Phoenix, AZ 85018

602-852-9500
602-852-9503 (fax)

www.bullpublishing.com

Photo captions:

Page 1: An official's armband from the 1956 NASCAR season.

Page 2-3: February 21, 1959. The pace lap for a 25-mile race held the day before the inaugural Daytona 500. Note the No. 43 convertible of Richard Petty in the top row, third from left.

Page 5: During the early 1970s, Sears sold this NASCAR theme fabric which was used for curtains and bedspreads.

Page 6: This standardized program for the NASCAR convertible circuit is typical of those issued by many short tracks during the mid-1950s through the 1962 season.

Page 7: This pin-back button of Joe Weatherly was sold at Darlington Raceway during the early 1960s.

WORLD 600
GRAND
EA
PIT
12
SEARS
STEEL-BELTED RADIAL TIRES
17
union 76
ON 500
10

NAS CAR

Official Program   50c

N<u>o</u> 102281

National Convertible Circuit

CONTENTS

Foreword
BY RICHARD PETTY

I've been collecting stuff all my life. I've got toys and trains and stuff I had when I was a kid. I collected my personal stuff and I collected stuff about racing in general. You name it, if it was around a race track I've probably got it-magazines, programs, newspaper clippings, pictures. We've got roomfuls of it.

I have the first T-shirt that was ever made on a race car driver, and that was me. Back in 1964 everybody had plain white T-shirts. Mine had my name and a picture of the car. We started making racing hats with the car on it. We cut a lot of new ground on all that souvenir stuff. We were collectors, but we were opportunists, too. We'd say, "Let's try this and see if it will work." A bunch of our stuff *didn't* work, I'll put it that way, but we didn't mind trying new things. At that time racing was not big enough to attract outside people to make things, it had to be done from the inside. Now it doesn't have to be done from the inside because there are so cotton-pickin' many people out there thinking up these ideas, parlaying money and business off the race cars.

Back then I remember it made you feel good to walk into a store and see one of your products, a race car or a picture or whatever. Now it's nothing. If you walk into a store and they haven't got something about racing you just turn around and leave!

The way everything's expanding I don't see the collectibles industry slowing or shooting itself in the foot. The good manufacturers are going to survive. And if those jacklegs who come in and try to make off with it don't do the right job, they're not going to last. And the deal when you're collecting is knowing or thinking you know which ones are going to be stable and which ones are not.

I think that with the Fiftieth Anniversary deal, NASCAR will educate a lot of new fans so that they'll know where we started. Because we're on the inside, we'd feel better if more fans knew some of our history. They need to know that we started with strictly stock stock cars. They were cars right off the street. We just took the hub caps and mufflers off, put numbers on them, and went racing.

Pure competition is what has made NASCAR so successful. These cats are racing all the time, whether they're racing for twentieth or tenth or first or whatever. And of all the sports out there, I think people can relate better to the drivers and

Above: Lee Petty hands his son a drink during a pit stop in the 1966 running of the Rebel 400 at Darlington. Richard won the race. Opposite: Richard Petty's first Daytona 500 victory was front page news in 1964. Lower: Richard on the starting grid in 1969.

cars and the overall deal in racing than they can in any other sport. Racing is very family-oriented. Whenever you see pictures of the drivers or crews, you often see their kids and their wives with them. If fans couldn't relate to us, and no one was going to the races, the collectibles and memorabilia wouldn't be worth anything.

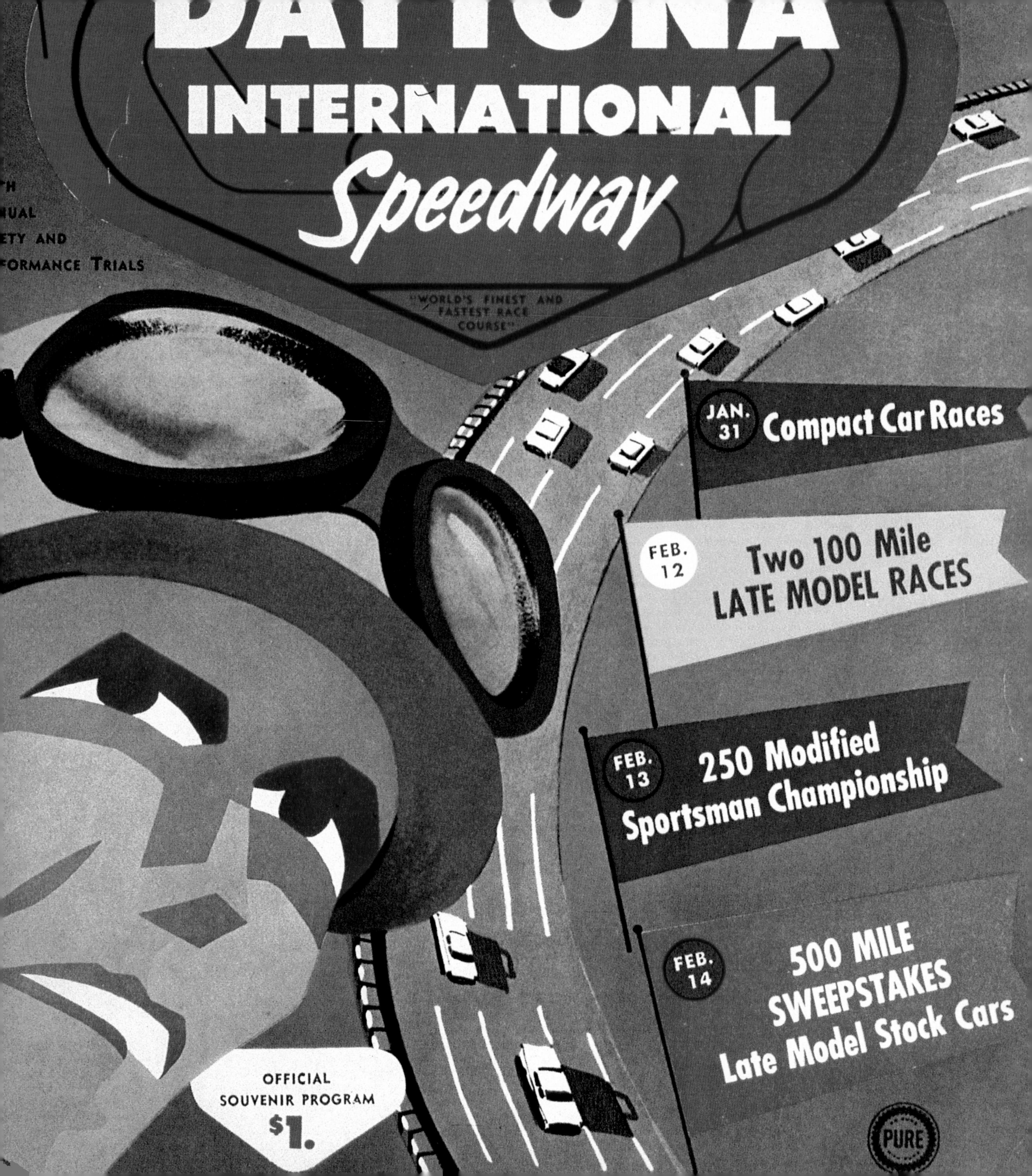

DAYTONA INTERNATIONAL *Speedway*

"WORLD'S FINEST AND FASTEST RACE COURSE"

TH
NUAL
ETY AND
FORMANCE Trials

JAN. 31 Compact Car Races

FEB. 12 Two 100 Mile LATE MODEL RACES

FEB. 13 250 Modified Sportsman Championship

FEB. 14 500 MILE SWEEPSTAKES Late Model Stock Cars

OFFICIAL SOUVENIR PROGRAM $1.

PURE

WORKING PRESS PASS
Daytona Beach STOCK CAR RACES
SATURDAY FEB. 20 1954
ISSUED TO
PAPER OR RADIO STATION

CHAPTER 1

Collecting Basics

Since the first stock car race on the sands of Daytona Beach, Florida, in March, 1936, fans have purchased souvenirs. While memories may fade, these souvenirs become memorabilia that race fans cherish as mementos of race events.

In the early days of stock car racing, few race fans thought of souvenirs as collectibles. Programs and tickets were simply part of being at the race. Sometimes they were saved and put into scrapbooks along with newspaper clippings about the race. Other times they were discarded or tossed into a drawer and forgotten. After all, who would have thought anyone would collect these items one day?

Until only a few years ago there was no organized hobby for collecting auto racing memorabilia. It is not surprising, therefore, that there is a lot of confusion among collectors about the basic terminology and the definition of "memorabilia" and "collectibles."

Opposite: This program from the Second Annual Daytona 500 in 1960 is actually harder to find than the inaugural edition, but demand for the historic 1959 inaugural program makes it a more valuable item to NASCAR collectors.

It has been said that memorabilia is collected, while collectibles are bought. When a new collectible comes out, it is purchased by a race fan at a retail outlet. Memorabilia, on the other hand, is much more difficult to find, often requiring time-consuming searches. To the veteran collector of racing items, memorabilia refers to older items that were not produced with the intention of being collected and includes programs, ticket stubs, credentials, posters, pins, rule books, buttons, and badges.

Collectibles, on the other hand, refers to more recently manufactured items that are specifically made to be collected, such as cards and diecast toys. These items are offered to hobbyists for the purpose of collecting, often in order to collect a complete set. Of course, there are exceptions, and the terms memorabilia and collectibles are often used interchangeably. After all, collectibles will eventually become memorabilia. And, memorabilia is collectible.

FIFTH ANNUAL
DAYTONA
FIRECRACKER
400

JULY 4, 1963

TINY LUND
Winner
1963 DAYTONA "500"

DAYTONA *International* SPEEDWAY
DAYTONA BEACH, FLORIDA
The World's Finest and Fastest Speedway
OFFICIAL SOUVENIR PROGRAM / Price $1.00

Left: Tiny Lund won the 1963 Daytona 500 and was featured on the cover of the Firecracker 400 program in July of that same year. Lund had rescued Marvin Panch from a burning car during a sports car race at Daytona early in 1963, and was rewarded with Panch's ride in the 500. Lund was later killed at Talladega.

Opposite: A variety of Southern 500 ticket brochures from the 1970s and 1980s. These fold-out flyers are colorful display items that have become popular among collectors. On the upper left is a 1981 ticket brochure, which shows Terry Labonte in victory lane after winning the 1980 Southern 500, his first NASCAR Winston Cup victory.

The term souvenir most often refers to merchandise sold at the track on race day, such as T-shirts, hats, pins, patches, and other items that don't usually have value to serious collectors. Don't be confused by the terminology, however. Whether you like old memorabilia or new collectibles, the hobby offers plenty for every race fan.

The collectibles segment of the hobby has blossomed into a multimillion dollar industry in recent years. Many longtime collectors prefer old racing memorabilia and reject collectibles as contrived and over-produced. However, the majority of NASCAR fans have embraced collectibles much the same way fans of other sports embraced card sets and other items related to their favorite sport.

This book features a wide array of racing memorabilia and collectibles, including many items seldom seen by even the most experienced collectors. There is tremendous variety in the historic racing artifacts that collectors look for, and this variety is the basis of today's collectible hobby. From the infancy of stock car racing in the 1930s on the sands of Daytona Beach to today's

DARLINGTON RACEWAY
SOUTHERN 500
LABOR DAY
SEPTEMBER 7
12 NOON

1980 SOUTHERN 500 WINNER
TERRY LABONTE

McLeod Industries 150
International Sedan Race
September 5   3:00 P.M.

Noon, Monday, September 5, 1983
DARLINGTON INTERNATIONAL RACEWAY
SOUTHERN 500
Winston Cup Series

The Granddaddy of Stock Car Racing

ALSO:
THE KOMFORT KOACH 150
3 pm, Saturday, September 3, 1983
THE DARLINGTON 250
2 pm, Sunday, September 4, 1983

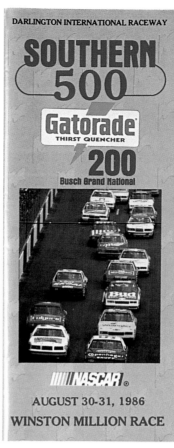

DARLINGTON INTERNATIONAL RACEWAY
SOUTHERN 500

Gatorade
THIRST QUENCHER

200
Busch Grand National

//// **NASCAR** ®

AUGUST 30-31, 1986
WINSTON MILLION RACE

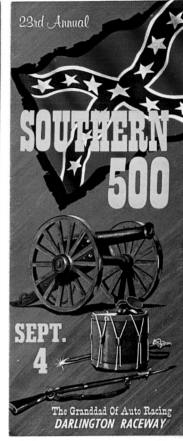

23rd Annual
SOUTHERN 500

SEPT. 4

The Granddad Of Auto Racing
DARLINGTON RACEWAY

DARLINGTON INTERNATIONAL RACEWAY
SOUTHERN 500
too tough to tame

PONTIAC WINNERS CIRCLE

SATURDAY,
AUGUST 31,
1 p.m.

200 //// **NASCAR** ©

SUNDAY, SEPTEMBER 1, 1985

DARLINGTON RACEWAY

SEPT 4
12:00
NOON
SOUTHERN 500

BABY GRANDS
SAT., SEPT. 2
3 P.M.

DARLINGTON RACEWAY
SOUTHERN 500
LABOR DAY
SEPTEMBER 6
12 NOON

McLeod Industries 150
International Sedan Race
September 4   3:00 p.m.

DARLINGTON RACEWAY
SOUTHERN 500
LABOR DAY
SEPTEMBER 3
12 NOON

BABY GRAND
SANDLAPPER 150
SAT., SEPT. 1, 3:00 P.M.

superspeedways, the sport has produced many great memories. Collecting is a way to acknowledge and preserve stock car racing's great heritage.

Origins of the Hobby

Although auto racing is America's most popular spectator sport, collecting motorsports memorabilia has only recently come into its own. There are several pioneers of the hobby who deserve recognition. The first major collector of racing memorabilia was Lawson Diggett of Ormond Beach, Florida. An enthusiast of automobiles in general and racing in particular, he witnessed the evolution of speed events at Daytona for over a half century. From the land speed record attempts of the 1920s to the phenomenal growth of NASCAR and Daytona International Speedway, Diggett saved everything related to racing he could get his hands on.

By the time he passed away, Diggett had amassed tens of thousands of books, magazines, tickets, posters, programs, newspapers, and photographs—virtually everything associated with racing at

Daytona Beach.

His interest in racing wasn't limited to collecting. Diggett also hand carved models of virtually every significant race car to compete at Daytona Beach and built an enormous diorama of Daytona Beach's famed boardwalk as it appeared in the 1930s. Much of his collection is now on display at the Halifax Historical Society Museum in Daytona Beach.

Bill Tuthill was another pioneer of auto racing memorabilia collecting. As one of the founding fathers of NASCAR and a promoter of racing events in New England, Tuthill's keen sense of history led him to open the Birthplace of Speed Museum just south of Daytona Beach. This attraction was a mainstay of race fans until it closed in the early 1970s.

While Tuthill is best known for rescuing the famed Bluebird land speed record car of the 1930s from a junkyard in England, he also managed to save a tremendous collection of racing memorabilia. Tuthill recognized that these items were an important way of preserving and documenting racing history. Most of his collection was eventually acquired by NASCAR's archives department. The Bluebird is now displayed at the Daytona USA attraction.

In Indianapolis, Indiana, Ron Plew had a similar passion. He amassed the largest Indianapolis 500 collection ever, obtaining samples of every program and ticket, plus thousands of other items. Most of his collection was purchased by other Indianapolis collectors after his death in 1985.

Indy collectors are perhaps the best organized in the motorsports collecting hobby. Opened in 1909, the Indianapolis Motor Speedway (IMS) has hosted the "Greatest Spectacle in Racing" since 1911. Since the first 500 that year, IMS has produced the most beautiful tickets, credentials, badges, and buttons ever designed for a sports event.

In 1979, the first national show devoted to racing memorabilia took place in downtown Indianapolis the day before the Indy 500. Nearly two decades later, this show, the National Auto Racing Memorabilia Expo, has grown to be one of the largest sports memorabilia shows in North America. Collectors of all types of racing memorabilia, NASCAR included, make this a must-see event for racing hobbyists.

A pit badge from the 1957 Southern 500 at Darlington depicting a Firestone tire. This is one of the few metal pit badges ever issued for a NASCAR race, a practice made famous by Indianapolis Motor Speedway (this badge is nearly identical to the one used for the 1952 Indianapolis 500). These pit badges had a pin back and a ribbon attached to the bottom.

Souvenir sales at NASCAR events are currently at record levels. T-shirts, hats, patches, pins, stickers, diecast cars, collector cards, and hundreds of other items can be purchased at virtually every NASCAR race. NASCAR fans are among the most loyal and dedicated sports fans in America, and the boom in sales of souvenirs and collectibles reflects this.

The stock car racing collectibles hobby began when nostalgia of all types grew in popularity during the 1970s. Old record albums, lunch boxes, and toys rapidly grew in stature as bonafide collectibles. Baseball cards became a major industry, and cards for other sports followed close behind. While the number of sports collectors flourished, however, there were only a handful of serious collectors of racing memorabilia.

The introduction of collector cards in the late 1980s by Maxx dramatically changed the racing hobby. The collector cards captured the interest of NASCAR fans who had wanted collectibles on the same level as those for other sports. Within a few years, several national companies—such as Pro Set, Upper Deck, Press Pass, and Finish Line—were producing card sets and other collectibles. The hobby grew quickly, reaching immense popularity by the early 1990s.

Diecast toys have been around for decades, but sales for stock car racing diecast toys have increased tremendously in recent years. Millions have been

Fireball *Roberts*

ICK CAR RACE
JUNE 8
IOLE SPEEDWAY

99

An autographed photo of Edward Glenn "Fireball" Roberts from early in his career. Roberts grew up in Daytona Beach and became a hometown hero by winning thirty-three Grand National races during his career. In 1964, Roberts was critically burned in a fiery wreck at Charlotte in May and died from infection on July 2. At left is an ERTL diecast car representing one of the modifieds that Roberts drove in the 1950s.

produced in a merchandising blitz on a scale rarely seen before. As the racing souvenir industry boomed, drivers and team owners reaped licensing revenues worth millions of dollars.

Interest in older auto racing memorabilia also grew rapidly, and it did not take long for the collector's ranks to swell into the thousands. Veteran collectors feel it is important for novice collectors to appreciate the historical value of the older items. The heritage of NASCAR racing goes back five decades, and the evolution of the sport is documented through the many older types of memorabilia shown in this book.

Where to Find Racing Memorabilia

Collecting items from the early days of NASCAR is truly a challenge. Because most older NASCAR items were produced in very small quantities and seldom saved, it usually takes many years to acquire the more rare programs, tickets, and other memorabilia.

Occasionally, used bookstores, antique shows, garage sales, or flea markets will turn up real finds. The best resource for finding early memorabilia is networking with other collectors and those involved in automotive-related hobbies.

Surprisingly, there is not a clearly defined geographic region for finding racing collectibles. Racing memorabilia turns up just about everywhere. While conventional wisdom may tell you

NASCAR items are most likely to be found in the southern United States, the fact is major events such as Daytona attracted a tremendous following of fans from the Northeast, Midwest and West Coast, who returned home with their NASCAR souvenirs.

Until the late 1980s, a race fan would be hard pressed to find racing collectibles and souvenirs anywhere other than at the race track. Now, racing merchandise and NASCAR items can be found in grocery stores, department stores, airport gift shops, toy stores, drug stores, and gas stations—just about anywhere. And the collectibles are updated every year when drivers change teams and teams change sponsors.

The racing collectibles hobby is now big business. Several hobby magazines devoted specifically to newer collectibles have started in recent years. Mail-order companies specializing in stock car racing collectibles and souvenirs have also emerged.

At NASCAR races, virtually every major team has its own souvenir hauler that sells a huge selection of collectibles. Before and after every race, thousands of fans can be seen buying items relating to their favorite drivers. In addition, NASCAR merchandise can be purchased from national cable television networks that feature racing collectible shows. Drivers are often guests on these shows, endorsing various items, many of which include their signatures.

For collectors of racing memorabilia, the Indianapolis show, held before the Indianapolis

ERTL RICHARD PETTY RACE SET

500, remains the biggest event of the year, but other shows geared toward racing collectibles have started around the country. On almost any given weekend throughout the year, there are several shows taking place devoted to racing collectibles.

Many collectors specialize in memorabilia pertaining to a particular driver. One of the most popular is Richard Petty, King of NASCAR racing. There are hundreds of Petty items. Shown on these pages are just a few: Petty STP pillow from 1974; Richard Petty playset from 1980; Richard Petty's "Rookie of the Year" trophy from 1959.

Displaying and Storing Collectibles

Race fans across the country—sometimes to the dismay of their spouses—have turned dens, garages, and even living rooms into motorsports memorabilia shrines.

Products for displaying racing memorabilia have become a thriving industry within the collectibles hobby. From showcases for diecast toys to binders and album pages for cards, the art of displaying collections has been refined in recent years. Because of the importance of maintaining a collection in excellent condition, it must be properly stored and protected from moisture, direct sunlight, dust, and excessive handling.

Many collectors have acquired so many items that they use computers to catalog their holdings. But no matter how many items a collector has or what is collected, displaying the collection is the best way to enjoy it. It is also a good idea to have photographs taken of your collection, not only for insurance purposes, but also to share with other collectors and race fans.

Determining Values

The most commonly asked question in the racing collectibles hobby is "What's it worth?" Determining values for most types of racing memorabilia is no different than for other types of antiques or collectibles. Rarity, demand, condition, and quality are the key factors in appraising how much an item is worth.

Rarity means just how scarce an item is in terms of quantity. Production runs and distribution determine rarity. As in any collectible hobby, the fewer produced, the harder they are to find. Unfortunately, the often abused term "limited edition" has become part of the hobby's lingo. In reality, many so-called limited editions are limited only to as many as the manufacturer can sell. Always be wary of new items that purport to be limited editions.

Richard Petty in 1964 at age 27. He won the first of his seven championships that year and dominated in the number of laps completed and laps led.

THIRD ANNUAL "DAYTONA 500"

and NASCAR WINTER SAFETY AND PERFORMANCE TRIALS

1961 RACE SCHEDULE

DAYTONA INTERNATIONAL SPEEDWAY

DAYTONA BEACH, FLORIDA

The World's Finest and Fastest Speedway

OFFICIAL RACING GASOLINE

PURE — BE SURE WITH PURE

NASCAR SANCTIONED

SPORTS CAR CLUB OF AMERICA

DEMAND is represented by the number of collectors who want a given item. For example, the demand for a program from the 1979 Daytona 500 is much higher than for a program from an obscure race during the 1952 NASCAR season, even though the older program is much more rare. By the same token, Richard Petty memorabilia is worth more than items relating to a little-known driver, even though Petty memorabilia is much more common. To some extent, demand is a popularity rating. Items from significant historical events tend to be in greater demand, so prices will be higher—supply and demand, pure and simple. Remember, rare doesn't necessarily mean valuable.

QUALITY comes into play especially with toys, models, and other three-dimensional items. The better the quality, the more likely an item will be in demand in the future. Graphics and use of color are important in determining the demand for posters and programs. Visual appeal is an important consideration.

CONDITION is a critical factor, especially with regard to older items. A program with a loose cover, yellowed pages, water stains, or a missing page is worth much less than the same program in excellent condition. Even a minor defect can detract from value, such as a card or photo with a slight crease. Packaging is also important. Diecast cars, plastic model kits, and racing slot car kits are usually worth more if they are in their original boxes.

Of course, any item is *really* worth no more than a person is willing to pay for it. Price guides are only an opinion. How much money changes hands is the true test of value, and this can vary greatly from region to region.

This book is not a price guide. Most of the items shown have no set value. When buying or selling racing memorabilia, carefully research the items and talk to more experienced collectors before making a decision.

Appreciating Racing History

To fully appreciate stock car racing memorabilia, the collector should know the history of the sport. The first auto race in the United States took place in Chicago in 1895. The cars that took part in that event were indeed completely stock automobiles, raced as delivered from their manufacturers.

While there were many events for stock cars in the years that followed, the first major stock car race took place at Daytona Beach in 1936. This event attracted one of the most diverse fields of drivers ever assembled. Indianapolis winner "Wild" Bill Cummings, sports car racing pioneer Sam Collier, and midget car racing star Bill Schindler joined a field of rough and tough Southern stock car racers. Among them was a lanky young man who had recently moved to Daytona Beach from Maryland. His name was Bill France.

Up until World War II, stock car racing flourished in the southern United States but remained

A program from the 1980 Southeastern 400 at Bristol. The cover shows Dale Earnhardt in victory lane after winning the 1979 event, his first NASCAR Winston Cup victory. Earnhardt won five races during the 1980 season and captured his first Winston Cup championship.

Above left: The first rule book that NASCAR prepared in 1948 was a scant four pages. Rule books today are hundreds of pages long and are supplemented by technical bulletins issued throughout the season.

Above right: Stock car racing literature from the 1950s and 1960s is difficult to find, so special publications such as this booklet from Falstaff beer are in demand among racing memorabilia collectors. It previews the 1967 Southern 500 and was distributed free as a magazine insert.

relatively unorganized. It was during this period that the legendary moonshiners honed their driving skills on the dusty back roads of the South.

Auto racing ceased during World War II, but resumed in 1946. Daytona Beach, Florida, remained the focal point of stock car racing with its annual beach road race. In 1947, Bill France founded the National Association of Stock Car Automobile Racing (NASCAR) at a meeting in the Streamline Hotel in Daytona Beach. France carefully crafted an organization that featured close competition with cars the public easily recognized: Ford, Chevrolet, Hudson, Pontiac, Oldsmobile, and other American cars. That strategy continues today, as NASCAR has grown to become America's most successful form of auto racing.

During the 1950s, two events in stock car racing stood out from the rest: the Daytona Winter Classic on the famed beach road course, and the Southern 500 at Darlington in South Carolina. Both helped make NASCAR racing a nationally recognized sport. Aside from these two major events, NASCAR featured an ambitious schedule with a race on virtually every weekend of the year. Legendary drivers such as Fireball Roberts, Herb Thomas, Tim and Fonty Flock, Junior Johnson, and Joe Weatherly were among NASCAR's pioneer racers.

Bill France's dream of building a racing facility to rival Indianapolis became a reality in 1959 when he completed the Daytona International Speedway. This began the superspeedway era, and

The very rare and historic program from the first stock car racing event held on the sands of Daytona Beach in March, 1936. This event is considered the birthplace of modern stock car racing.

stock car racing would never be the same. The Daytona 500 instantly became the premier stock car race. Charlotte and Atlanta opened the following year. By the end of the 1960s, several other speedways had opened, including Rockingham, Pocono, Michigan, and Talladega. New stars earned their reputation on these high speed ovals—Richard Petty, David Pearson, Bobby Allison and Cale Yarborough, to name just a few.

Television coverage and multimillion dollar sponsorship deals boosted stock car racing to new levels in the 1980s. Dale Earnhardt, Darrell Waltrip, and Tim Richmond ushered in a new era of flamboyant NASCAR drivers who earned legions of loyal fans. And in 1994 NASCAR became part of the world's most famous track when stock car racing began at the Indianapolis Motor Speedway.

After the formation of NASCAR in 1947, stock car racing's popularity grew rapidly and manufacturers took an interest in racing stock automobiles. Other organizations began sanctioning stock car racing. The American Automobile Association (AAA) held several major events during the early 1950s. The United States Auto Club (USAC) took over the AAA racing division in 1956 and continued to sanction stock car racing through the 1970s.

The International Motor Contest Association (IMCA) originally sanctioned sprint car racing primarily in the Midwest, but they also added a stock car racing division. The Automobile Racing Club of America (ARCA) and other groups such as ASA (American Speed Association) continue to sanction stock car racing today.

Memorabilia from these organizations does not have the same appeal to collectors as NASCAR. Similarly, other divisions of NASCAR do not have the appeal of the Grand National (now Winston Cup) division.

The north turn of the famous Daytona Beach course during the inaugural stock car race in 1936. The race was run on a handicap basis with smaller engine displacement cars given a head start. The winner was Milt Marion, who drove a Ford V-8. Finishing sixth was a young man named Bill France (left), who had recently moved to Daytona Beach from Maryland. He would go on to create NASCAR and build both Daytona and Talladega speedways.

Why Collect Stock Car Racing Memorabilia?

People collect stamps, coins, baseball cards, beer cans—you name it, someone collects it. NASCAR fans are among the most loyal in sports, so it is only natural that their love of racing fuels their desire for collectibles.

Whatever your passion, you should collect for the enjoyment of it and try to avoid the speculative nature of collectibles. A properly displayed collection of racing memorabilia is a great conversation piece and a welcome escape from the everyday pressures of life.

But of course, racing collectibles can be a lucrative investment. Older memorabilia has become extremely valuable in recent years. Some race programs from Darlington that sold for fifty cents back in the 1950s are now selling for well over $100. The same holds true for plastic model kits of NASCAR cars from the early 1970s, particularly the early MPC kits. Old NASCAR memberships, pins, yearbooks, armbands, and rule books have increased dramatically in value.

Many collectibles, although only a few years old, also have become quite valuable, such as the first Maxx set for certain diecast toys from the late 1980s. As new race fans enter the hobby every year, the demand for the more desirable collectibles grows and prices skyrocket.

And remember, stock car racing has been around only since 1936, and NASCAR since 1947. Other types of racing date back much further. The Indy 500 was first held in 1911, and a program from that event can sell for over $2,000! It stands to reason that as NASCAR continues to grow, so will the value of its collectibles.

Meeting other collectors is another good reason to take part in the racing collectibles hobby. Chances are you will establish lifelong relationships with other race fans who have become collectors.

Nostalgia is perhaps the main reason people collect. Racing collectibles help people turn back the clock, often to the days of their youth, to bring back great memories.

What to Collect

There are many categories of racing memorabilia and collectibles. This book illustrates the tremendous variety of items that race fans collect, ranging from rare programs dating back to the first year of NASCAR in 1948 to diecast toys sold by the millions today.

Some race fans collect items related to their favorite driver, including uniforms, helmets, autographs, and photographs. Others collect memorabilia relating to certain tracks or races. Many race fans limit their collecting endeavors to specific categories of memorabilia, such as programs, tickets, or credentials. Others prefer post cards, autographs, patches, and decals. The beauty of racing collectibles is that they run the gamut of interests and budgets.

Daytona Beach Evening News

(C) 1983 News-Journal Corp.

"Give me the liberty to know, to utter, and to argue freely according to conscience above all other liberties."—Milton

VOL. 55 NO. 38   MONDAY, FEBRUARY 14, 1983   ·S   25 CENTS

Monday's Report

Inside Today

...In The Nation

Congressional leaders are focusing their efforts this week on legislation to create emergency government jobs, but will find themselves confronted with rival plans to ease the nation's high unemployment ... **Page 3A**

Despite objections from the tobacco industry, a loose coalition of congressmen, medical officials and consumer groups is seeking legislation aimed at requiring cigarettes be made less likely to ignite fires ... **Page 3A**

...In Florida

Cale Crashes Car; Hits 200.503 MPH

Two Time Daytona 500 Winner Cale Yarborough drove his Chevrolet Monte Carlo to what is believed to be a stock car racing record this morning at Daytona International Speedway before a wind gust flipped the car end over end.

Yarborough, of Timmonsville, S.C., escaped injury in the crash during qualifying for Sunday's Silver Anniversary Daytona 500. Moments later, track officials said his speed of 200.503 wouldn't qualify for Sunday's race because his car was demolished.

The veteran driver said he will return to Charlotte, N.C., where he has another Monte Carlo ready to race. He'll run it in one of Thursday's two 125 mile runs to qualify for the 500. Speedway officials said Yarborough would have had to run Sunday's race in the same car in which he qualified today in order for the speed to hold up.

Just after Yarborough's crash, Ricky Rudd drove his Monte Carlo at a speed recorded at 198.864, which put him in the pole position for the 500 Sunday, as of mid-morning.Second at that time was Geoff

Newspapers, especially those from Daytona Speed Weeks are popular among collectors and historians alike. This 1983 issue shows Cale Yarborough's famous accident after breaking the 200-mph barrier in qualifying. Despite the accident, he won the Daytona 500 that year.

A Cale Yarborough ceramic Sippin' Whiskey decanter. The roof comes off to reveal an opening for pouring liquor. This car is modeled after the Junior Johnson–prepared Kar Kare Chevrolet that won four races during the 1973 season.

It is important for new collectors to understand and appreciate older memorabilia. This memorabilia is the foundation of the collecting hobby, and knowing its history—where it all came from and why it is valued—provides a foundation for understanding the importance of what is available today. Although collecting artifacts from the early days of NASCAR is a challenge because of their scarcity, they represent a historical link to contemporary items.

Most early memorabilia—programs, tickets, posters, and credentials—is made of paper. Programs are the most popular form of memorabilia. Enthusiasts often attempt to find a complete set of programs from a major event such as the Daytona 500, Southern 500, or World 600. Others collect programs from every event of the year (keep in mind NASCAR ran up to sixty-two Grand National races in a single year!). Some race fans only collect programs from races that their

favorite drivers won. Programs are also an excellent source of historical data.

Tickets and credentials are rapidly growing in popularity. Most serious collectors attempt to find at least one credential from every Daytona 500, the premier stock car racing event.

While paper items are very popular, they are often difficult to display because of the fragile nature of older paper. That is not the case with models and diecast toys. Their three-dimensional nature makes them ideal to place on shelves or in special cabinets.

With the introduction of Maxx Cards in 1988, the racing collectibles hobby exploded. Hundreds of card sets flooded the market, and not long after that, diecast cars took over as the most popular segment of the hobby. An incredible array of diecast Winston Cup cars in a variety of scales has been joined by diecast haulers, trucks, and other toys. Since sponsors and drivers often change from year to year, there are constantly new issues for enthusiasts to add to their collection. The diecast collecting hobby has swept NASCAR fans by storm, and annual sales are in the tens of millions of dollars.

It is this segment of the hobby, however, that collectors need to be the most careful about. During the early stages of the race card and diecast hobby, there was a great deal of misinformation. Some dealers, distributors, and hobby publications made claims regarding production quantities and values that were grossly inaccurate. Some of the published price guides were based more on wishful thinking than on a realistic assessment of supply and demand. Many novice collectors paid premium prices for items that were not worth such an investment.

A majority of the new collectibles on the market are produced in such large quantities that it is unlikely they will appreciate in value, even in the

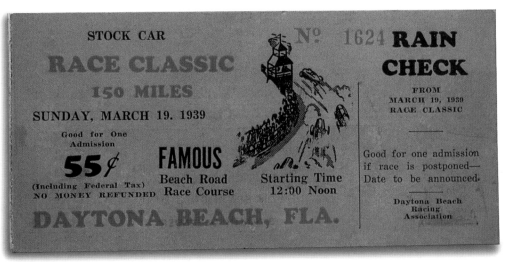

A ticket stub from the 1939 beach road races in Daytona Beach, before the formation of NASCAR. Starting times for races on the beach had to be adjusted depending on when it was low tide.

This special display poster was distributed on a limited basis by Ford dealers in 1963 and features the 1962 Daytona 500 with Fireball Roberts crossing the finish line. This artwork was also used by Pepsi for its ad on the back cover of the 1963 Daytona 500 program.

A poster from the 1977 Atlanta 500 showing NASCAR legend David Pearson and the famous Wood Brothers pit crew in action. Pearson was the defending champion of this race and won ten races during the 1976 season. This poster design was also used for the program cover that year. Few NASCAR tracks issue event posters today.

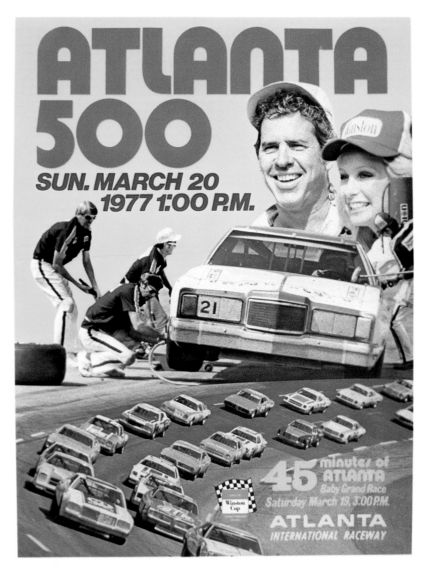

distant future. Learn from veteran collectors and read as much as you can about the hobby. Go to racing collectible shows and compare prices before going overboard in your collecting endeavors. If you are looking at collectibles as an investment, it is essential that you gather as much information as possible before making purchases. "Let the Buyer Beware" certainly holds true in this hobby.

Older memorabilia is probably the best investment. Programs, yearbooks, credentials, and ticket stubs can still be purchased for relatively reasonable prices compared to baseball and football memorabilia of the same age. But as the stock car racing collectibles hobby grows, finding these already scarce items will become more and more difficult.

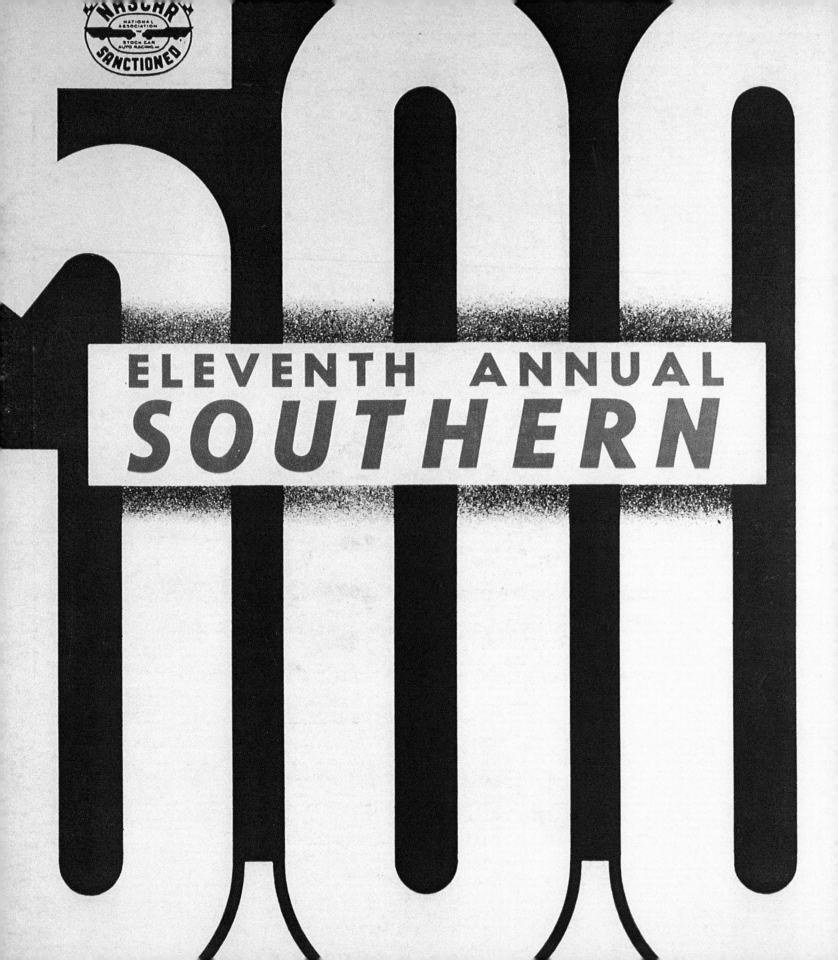

NASCAR SANCTIONED
NATIONAL ASSOCIATION STOCK CAR AUTO RACING

ELEVENTH ANNUAL
SOUTHERN

500

CHAPTER 2

Programs

Souvenir programs are the most popular paper items collected by race fans. The photographs, articles, and advertisements create a historical record that captures a moment in time and preserves it for future generations. Looking through the pages of a program, a race fan can travel back in time to relive great moments.

Souvenir programs have been around since the beginning of professional sports events. The old adage "You can't tell the players without a scorecard" made official baseball programs a tradition starting in the 1860s. Now, every major sporting event—football, basketball, golf, tennis, hockey—publishes some type of official program.

Auto racing programs have been a key part of the sport from the beginning. America's first great international racing event, the Vanderbilt Cup Race of 1904, had a beautiful string-bound program. Most programs from the first decade of the century were usually elaborate, well-designed publications.

Indianapolis has had impressive programs dating back to its opening in 1909. Many pre-World War II racing programs have beautiful cover art that make them spectacular display items today.

For board track events, the 1920s featured some of the most spectacular racing programs ever produced. Board track programs from the 1930s, however, were generally more modest in design and cost, as America dealt with the Great Depression. Programs seldom cost more than twenty-five cents during the early years. That price has now escalated to over ten dollars for contemporary programs at some Winston Cup events.

Above: Known as stock car racing's Golden Boy for his blond hair and movie-star looks, Fred Lorenzen was featured on the cover of the 1964 Atlanta 500 program. Lorenzen was the defending champion of the Atlanta 500, having edged out Fireball Roberts the previous year. He won eight of the sixteen races he started in 1964.

Opposite: The rather basic cover of the 1960 Southern 500 program at Darlington. Buck Baker won the race, finishing just ahead of 1960 Grand National Champion Rex White. The Southern 500 is the oldest NASCAR superspeedway event and is a favorite of many collectors.

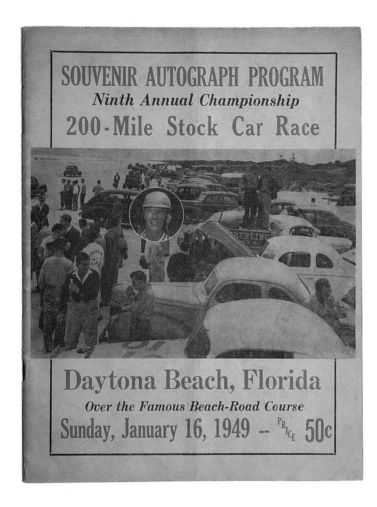

SOUVENIR AUTOGRAPH PROGRAM
Ninth Annual Championship
200-Mile Stock Car Race

Daytona Beach, Florida
Over the Famous Beach-Road Course
Sunday, January 16, 1949 -- PRICE 50c

Left: A program from a 1949 stock car race at Daytona Beach, one of the earliest events sanctioned by NASCAR. Note it states "Ninth Annual," referring to pre-NASCAR events on the beach course beginning in 1936. There were no races during World War II.

Opposite: Tim Flock in car 47A roared past the spinning car of Tom Herzberg (at left) on his way to victory in the 1956 NASCAR Modified race at Daytona Beach.

Stock car racing programs have evolved over the years from single-page handouts to elaborate, full-color, 300-page publications. By collecting programs, a NASCAR fan can follow the evolution of this great sport, creating a paper history that also serves as a great reference library.

Since a relatively small number of programs were sold at each early event, and even fewer survived the passage of time, programs are an enticing collectible. Programs from the early years of stock car racing before the formation of NASCAR are quite rare, especially those from Daytona Beach. Most of these early programs were neither elaborate nor particularly attractive, and only a few exist today.

Most early stock car racing programs were only four or eight pages and simply listed the entries along with a plethora of local ads. There were seldom photographs. Not surprisingly, since they weren't intended to be saved, few were.

The first NASCAR-sanctioned "Strictly Stock" Grand National race was held in Charlotte, North Carolina, on June 19, 1949. The program from this event is hard to find and often commands a high price when offered for sale. However, the most desirable programs from the early years of NASCAR are from the Daytona Beach Classics and the Southern 500 during the 1950s.

Though stock car racing at Daytona began in 1936 (there were up to four events per year in

Below: Daytona's annual February Speed Weeks tradition began in 1950 with the first Daytona Beach Classics. This program is among the rarest of all NASCAR programs, and is the only one with a black-and-white cover.

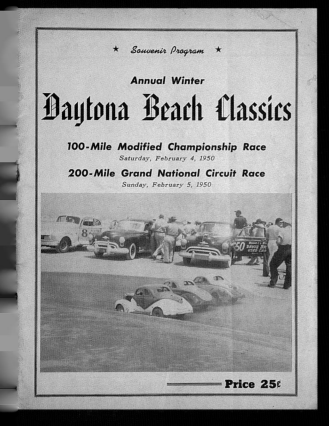

★ *Souvenir Program* ★

Annual Winter

Daytona Beach Classics

100-Mile Modified Championship Race
Saturday, February 4, 1950

200-Mile Grand National Circuit Race
Sunday, February 5, 1950

——— **Price 25¢**

Souvenir Program

Eighth Annual **NASCAR** *International*

SAFETY AND PERFORMANCE TRIALS AND RACES

DAYTONA BEACH FLA.

PLYMOUTH — OFFICIAL PACE CAR
INTERNATIONAL SAFETY AND PERFORMANCE TRIALS
DAYTONA BEACH, FLORIDA

Price **75¢**

SPEED TRIALS . . . . . . February 3-13, 1957
QUALIFYING TRIALS . . . . February 14, 1957
STOCK CAR RACES . . . . February 15, 16, 17, 1957

ANNUAL WINTER

Daytona Beach Classics

00-Mile Sportsmen's and Modified Stock Car Race — Saturday, February 9, 1952
00-Mile Grand National Circuit Race — Sunday, February 10, 1952
50¢

ANNUAL WINTER

Daytona Beach Classics

Golden Anniversary
Daytona Beach Speed Events
1903 - 1953

100-Mile Modified and Sportsmen's Stock Car Race
SATURDAY, FEBRUARY 14, 1953 - 1:45 P. M.
DIRECTOR
BILL FRANCE 160-MILE GRAND NATIONAL CIRCUIT RACE
PRICE **50¢**

Above: The 1957 Daytona Beach program featured the Plymouth convertible pace car on the cover with Bill France seated on the far right. The Kiekhaefer Outboards Chrysler team can be seen leading the pack into the north turn in the photographs on the cover.

Far left: The cover of the 1952 program shows the first lap of the 1951 race. Marshall Teague, Daytona resident and defending race champion, is shown with Herb Thomas, the 1951 NASCAR Grand National champion.

Left: The year 1953 marked the fiftieth anniversary of racing on Daytona Beach, which started with land speed record attempts. The top photo on the cover shows a spectacular view of the north turn.

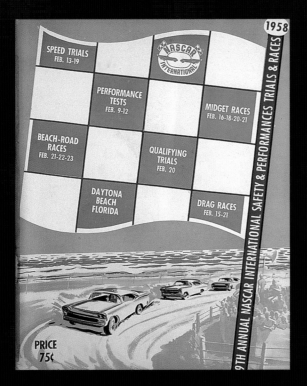

Above: Two bathing beauties holding a Speed Week poster grace the cover of the 1954 Daytona program. The poster they are holding would be a valuable collector's item today. In the background are scenes of the previous year's races.

Above left: A program from the last stock car race on Daytona Beach in 1958. The following year, NASCAR moved ten miles west to the new superspeedway built by Bill France. Motorcycle races were held on the beach in 1959, but they also moved to the speedway.

A program from the historic inaugural Southern 500 at Darlington in 1950. The Labor Day classic at Darlington was NASCAR's premier race throughout the 1950s. This program ranks among the most historic in stock car racing history, but it is often misidentified by collectors as the name "Southern 500" was not used anywhere on the cover.

subsequent years), the Winter Classics officially began in 1950 when Daytona went to its traditional format for February Speed Weeks. Performance trials and a full schedule of NASCAR events took place, culminating in the Grand National division. The sight and sound of these cars thundering down Highway A1A and onto the sands of Daytona Beach was tremendously exciting and can never be duplicated. For stock car racing historians and collectors, this early era is the most spectacular and its memorabilia is in great demand.

The first Daytona Classic program from 1950 is very rare and one of the most difficult NASCAR programs to find. It contains only twenty-four black-and-white pages and measures 9 by 12 inches. Daytona Beach programs grew steadily in page count, and the 1953 program celebrated the fiftieth anniversary of the first speed trials held on the beach. The early Daytona NASCAR programs were designed by Houston Lawing, who set the standard for stock car racing

programs for many years to come. In 1954 the Daytona programs went to a more standard 8½-by-11-inch size. These programs are not only rare and in great demand, they also are quite informative, containing numerous photographs and statistical data that is nearly impossible to find anywhere else.

In 1958, the final Daytona Winter Classic (officially titled the Ninth Annual NASCAR International Safety and Performance Trials and Races) ended a great tradition of racing on the beach. Subsequent races were held at the new Daytona International Speedway, beginning a new era in racing.

The first Southern 500 was held in 1950 at the new Darlington Raceway in South Carolina. This was the first big speedway constructed for stock car racing and its annual Labor Day event quickly became the sport's premier race. The program from Darlington's first 500 has a yellow cover with an aerial photograph of the track, but nowhere does it say "Southern 500." This program is not as difficult to find as one might expect due to its large press run, but it is quite valuable because of its historical significance.

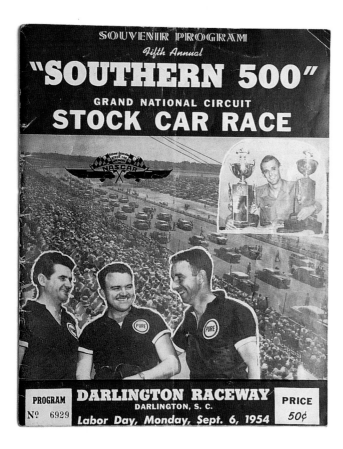

opened in 1959, Southern 500 programs continue to be popular among collectors. Interestingly, the Thirteenth Annual Southern 500 in 1962 was not called as such because the promoter was superstitious. The race was instead known as the Twelfth Renewal.

While the most historic of all stock car racing programs are those from the beach racing era at Daytona and the Southern 500, the most popular programs are those from the Daytona 500. For virtually every NASCAR collector, Daytona 500 programs are the centerpiece of their collection. Like World Series programs for baseball collectors and Super Bowl programs for football collectors, the Daytona 500 represents the most important event of the season.

The inaugural Daytona 500 program from 1959 is the single most sought-after program of all. Not only is it the first program from the sport's most important event, it also represents the begin-

The original program from the second Southern 500 in 1951 at Darlington is quite rare, although unauthorized reproductions from the early 1980s look nearly identical to the original. (The photographs in the reprint are slightly darker than the original and the paper used for the reprint is heavier.) The following year, 1952, the Southern 500 program had a cover that was also used that year by several other events, making it one of the most difficult Darlington programs to identify.

The Southern 500 was stock car racing's Indianapolis 500 during the 1950s. Items from this era are quite scarce, and programs and other memorabilia—such as tickets and credentials—are now very popular among serious NASCAR collectors.

Even though the Southern 500 was demoted in stature when Daytona International Speedway

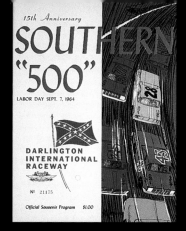

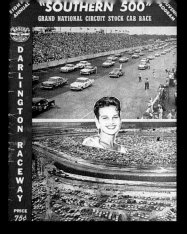

First Annual

Official Souvenir Program

NASCAR
NATIONAL ASSOCIATION FOR STOCK CAR AUTO RACING, INC.
SANCTIONED

500 MILE
INTERNATIONAL SWEEPSTAKES
AND OTHER RACING EVENTS
Feb. 20, 21, 22 -1959

**10th Annual
Safety and
Performance Trials
Feb. 15-19, 1959**

**PRICE
$1⁰⁰**

Daytona International Speedway
"WORLD'S FASTEST AND FINEST RACE COURSE"
DAYTONA BEACH, FLORIDA

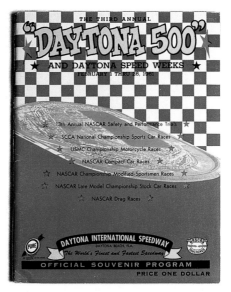

ning of the NASCAR superspeedway era.

In terms of rarity, the Second Annual Daytona 500 program from 1960 is more scarce, but it does not normally command the high prices that a 1959 program can attain, due to the historical importance of the inaugural program. This is a prime example of the fickle balance between demand and scarcity.

Daytona 500 programs have generally been the finest NASCAR programs in terms of quality, size, and content. Since 1974, Daytona 500 programs have had flat spines, known as perfect binding. Beginning in 1988, Daytona 500 programs have included a commemorative patch affixed to the program cover, a popular gimmick with little value to serious memorabilia collectors since these patches usually can be purchased separately.

Daytona 500 programs often sell out on race day, making even recent editions quite collectible. Not surprisingly, earlier years have increased in value as new collectors enter the hobby. Some Daytona 500 programs have become more valuable because of events that happened during the race. Richard Petty's first Daytona win in 1964 and the famous Pearson–Petty wreck at the finish

of the 1976 race have made these two programs in high demand.

Keep in mind that almost all NASCAR programs over the past three decades have had separate lineup sheets loosely inserted. These were usually available only with programs sold on race day. Collectors strive to obtain these inserts to make their programs complete.

Aside from Daytona, other major super speedway events are popular among NASCAR program collectors. Charlotte and Atlanta programs,

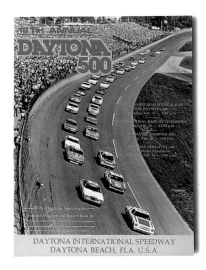

DAYTONA INTERNATIONAL SPEEDWAY
DAYTONA BEACH, FLA. U.S.A.

especially from the 1960s, are certainly worth collecting. Charlotte's World 600 programs have gained a following in recent years as Charlotte Motor Speedway continues to grow in stature. Interestingly, the first five World 600 programs from 1960 to 1964 have nearly identical cover art. The inaugural World 600 program had a white background, the following year's was cream-colored, and the next three had yellow backgrounds. Otherwise, these programs have the same cover design.

As in most sports, "first annual" events tend to be more valuable than those for subsequent years even if they are not rare. The First Annual Firecracker 250 at Daytona in 1959 and the First Annual Rebel 300 (the NASCAR convertible race) at Darlington in 1957 are among several first-edition programs that are quite difficult to find.

Another desirable first annual program is from the first Talladega 500 in 1969, which is infamous for being the "boycott race." Several leading drivers went on strike in a dispute with Bill France over the formation of a driver's union. With a few exceptions, the field consisted of little-known drivers. The race was won by Richard Brickhouse.

Weather conditions during a race can determine the value of programs and other event souvenirs. Programs from events plagued by rain tend to be more difficult to find since most were damaged by water or discarded at the track after the event was over.

Above left: The 1976 Daytona 500 program. This legendary race featured one of the greatest finishes in stock car racing history when Richard Petty and David Pearson crashed on the final turn of the last lap. Pearson's smashed Mercury managed to limp across the finish line to capture his only Daytona 500 victory.

Above center and right: The covers of the first four World 600 programs at Charlotte had identical artwork with only minor color variations. Shown here are the 1962 and 1963 editions.

Opposite: A 1962 Dixie 400 program. The cover shows the leading NASCAR stars of that era, with defending champion David Pearson the largest photograph. Rex White won the race that year, followed by Joe Weatherly and Marvin Panch.

OFFICIAL SOUVENIR PROGRAM

SALUTING ATLANTA'S WINNERS

THE *Dixie* 400

ATLANTA
INTERNATIONAL RACEWAY

FIREBALL ROBERTS

DAVE PEARSON

BOBBY JOHNS

BOB BURDICK

FRED LORENZEN

ATLANTA INTERNATIONAL RACEWAY

NASCAR SANCTIONED

ONE DOLLAR

OCTOBER · 28 · 1962

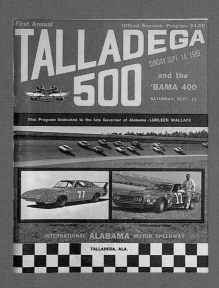

Above: A program from the first Talladega 500 in 1969. This race is infamous for being the "boycott race," in which Richard Petty led a strike by a newly formed driver's organization. Only a handful of regular drivers competed in the race, with the remainder of the field made up of relatively unknown drivers. Richard Brickhouse won the race.

Left: Richard Petty's pit crew waits for orders to drive his No. 43 Ford back to Randleman, North Carolina, after Petty and other members of the Professional Driver's Association announced they would not drive in the 1969 Talladega 500.

Below left: A program from the last NASCAR Convertible Division race ever held—The 1962 Rebel 300 at Darlington.

Below center: A program from the first annual Peach Blossom 500 at Rockingham's North Carolina Motor Speedway. Inaugural programs tend to be valued somewhat more than other years.

Below right: A program from Richard Petty's 200th career win—the 1984 Pepsi Firecracker 400. This race was recently selected as NASCAR's most historic event. Programs and other memorabilia from races that feature historic moments often become quite valuable.

Opposite: A 1962 Firecracker 250 program. The programs from Daytona's July Fourth race were printed in much smaller quantities than the Daytona 500 programs, however, demand for them is far less.

Far right: A program from the first Firecracker 250 at Daytona in 1959 (the distance was increased to 400 miles beginning in 1963). The race was originally scheduled to be an Indianapolis car race, but the track proved too dangerous for the open-wheel cars after George Amick and Marshall Teague were killed earlier in the year at the high-banked oval.

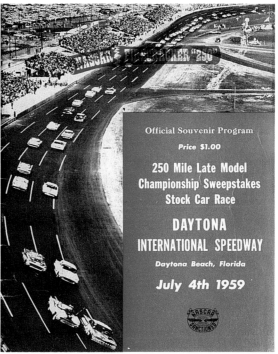

Programs from defunct tracks are often of interest to collectors. Riverside and Ontario are two California tracks that hosted NASCAR events over the years; however, most of these programs are not particularly rare. Other defunct tracks, such as Langhorne and Trenton, and inactive tracks such as Texas World Speedway, hosted several NASCAR Grand National races. These programs are an interesting addition to any collection. For tracks like these, the final program is often more valuable than the first program.

Until the NASCAR Grand National schedule was shortened significantly in 1971, races were held at short tracks all over the United States and Canada. Many of them were held at obscure, long-forgotten venues such as North Platte, Nebraska; Rapid City, South Dakota; Titusville-Cocoa Airport, Florida; Hanford, California; and Corbin, Kentucky. Literally hundreds of tracks around the country hosted Grand National races, and finding programs from these events is the toughest challenge for many collectors.

Most of these early NASCAR programs were small publications, hardly worth saving at the time. A few were quite elaborate for their day, such as the Detroit 250 programs. Souvenir programs from the early 1950s are the most difficult to find and there are even a few races for which programs are not known to exist.

NASCAR issued standardized programs for

many of the short track events from the 1950s through the early 1970s. For collectors, these programs often pose a challenge in determining which event they were from. These programs were magazine-style and basically identical except for the driver lineup insert. Pro football and basketball have done the same thing since the early 1970s. Fortunately, NASCAR event programs today are produced by their respective tracks and each has its own distinct style.

Programs for events held at unique locations or races with unusual results are desirable to collectors. For example, the only NASCAR Grand National race won by a foreign car took place in 1954 at the Linden Airport in New Jersey, when Al Keller drove a Jaguar to victory. This race was an experiment by NASCAR allowing certain foreign makes to compete. The program from this

Opposite: In 1951, The Detroit 250 was one of the few major NASCAR races held outside the southern United States. The colorful program prepared for the event was elaborate for its time.

Below left: These two 1952 Grand National programs from South Bend, Indiana, and West Palm Beach, Florida, are examples of generic publications. They are virtually identical inside and out.

Below: Many short tracks used generic programs like these from 1958. Although their covers are slightly different, the content inside is identical.

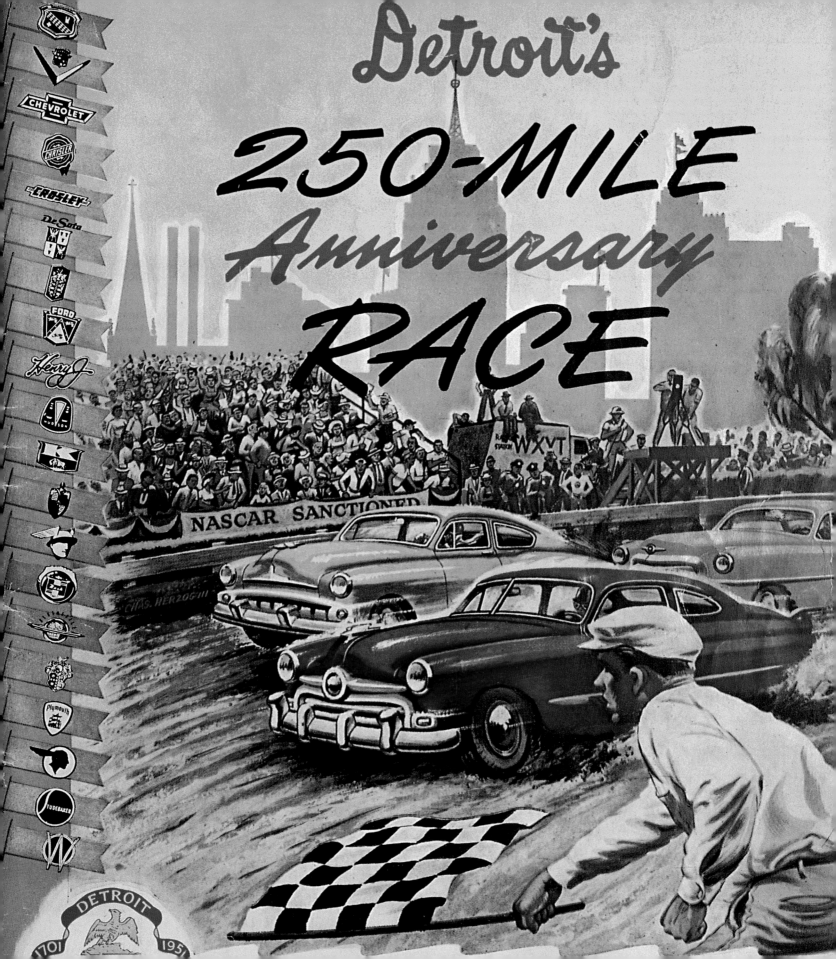

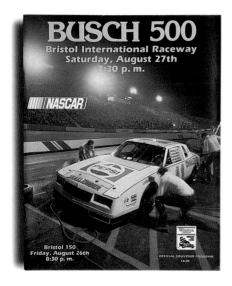
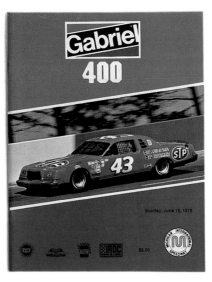
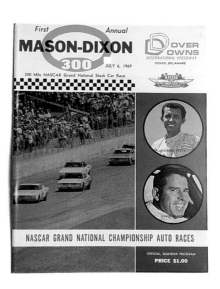

Programs from Bristol (1982), Michigan (1978), and Dover Downs (1969). Every NASCAR program has its own style, as reflected by the cover art. This makes program collecting a very enjoyable albeit challenging hobby, since many tracks sell out their programs on race day.

event is quite popular among both stock car and sports car racing memorabilia enthusiasts.

Richard Petty's first of 200 career wins occurred at the Charlotte Fairgrounds on February 28, 1960. A program from this event is more valuable than most other programs from that era because of its historical significance. The same will likely hold true for the program from the Southeastern 500 at Bristol on April 1, 1979, when Dale Earnhardt took his first career Winston Cup win.

In 1961, the Atlanta Motor Speedway had an Indy car race scheduled for July 9. Only a week before the event, the United States Auto Club

(USAC) canceled the race, calling the track unsafe for Indianapolis-type cars. NASCAR quickly moved in and sanctioned the Festival 250, organizing the stock car event in a matter of days. Not surprisingly, the program from this event is scarce due to the small press run.

One of the most unusual NASCAR Grand National races took place on November 17, 1963, at a three-mile road course in Augusta, Georgia, which was originally a road through a housing development. Part of the 1964 NASCAR season, the 510-mile race was eventually stopped after five hours, with Fireball Roberts winning by one lap. It was the first and only stock car race ever held there, and the program from the event is difficult to find. The very next race of the season took place at Jacksonville Speedway Park in Florida and it turned out to be a historic event. Buck Baker was flagged the winner, but a scoring discrepancy was discovered that may have intentionally short-changed

Wendall Scott two laps. Scott was later declared the winner, the first black driver to win a NASCAR stock car race.

Of course, the roots of NASCAR racing lie in hundreds of short tracks across the country, including Martinsville in Virginia, Fonda in New York, and North Wilkesboro, Bowman-Gray Stadium, Raleigh Speedway, Shelby Fairgrounds, and Asheville-Weaverville Speedway, all in North Carolina. Many collectors specialize in tracks in their particular state or region.

Additionally, some race fans collect programs from organizations that sanctioned stock car racing, such as the USAC and AAA. While some of these programs are of interest from a historical standpoint, few have value from a collecting standpoint compared to NASCAR programs.

Below left: The first and only Augusta 510 NASCAR road race in 1963 was held on the streets of a future housing development. Fireball Roberts won the race on the high-banked road course. Programs from one-race venues such as this are often very difficult to find.

Below center: This Festival 250 program was hastily prepared by Atlanta International Raceway in 1961. The race was scheduled to be a USAC Indianapolis car race but was canceled only two weeks prior and replaced by a NASCAR Grand National race.

Below right: A program from the NASCAR Grand National road race at the Linden, New Jersey, airport in 1954. It was the only NASCAR Grand National race ever won by a foreign car, a Jaguar driven by Al Keller.

№ 297

GARAGE PASS

DAYTONA
INTERNATIONAL
SPEEDWAY
DAYTONA BEACH
FLORIDA

Feb. 8-17, 1974

CHAPTER 3

Tickets & Credentials

For the price of admission, everyone at a racing event receives a souvenir worth keeping. Ticket stubs are the ultimate "I was there" collectible that is truly a limited edition.

Discarded in the past by most race fans soon after finding their seats, these little pieces of paper sometimes become worth their weight in gold. Others become racing history mementos with more sentimental significance than collecting value.

Ticket Stubs

Today, virtually everyone saves their ticket stubs. Small enough to put in a wallet or shirt pocket during the race, they can later be stored in an album or displayed in a frame.

The tradition of producing ticket stubs worthy of becoming collector's items was started by the Indianapolis Motor Speedway for the annual Indianapolis 500. Since the early 1920s, Indy 500 tickets have been colorful, ornate, and at times spectacular in their design. Beginning in 1948, the ticket's artwork featured the previous year's winner, a tradition that continues today. The Indy 500 tickets of the 1950s and 1960s are particu-

larly stunning collectibles, colorful and well designed. More recently, holograms, foil, and special inks and paper have been used. This not only frustrates would be counterfeiters, but continues to make the Indianapolis 500 tickets the most at-

Above right: Tracks used a large variety of credential styles during the 1960s. This window-style celluloid button was used by Daytona in 1961 along with a metal pit badge and paper credentials.

Opposite: Most NASCAR credentials and garage passes since the 1970s have resembled these from Daytona.

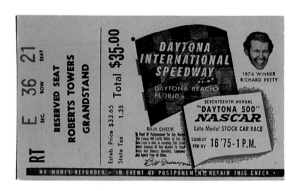

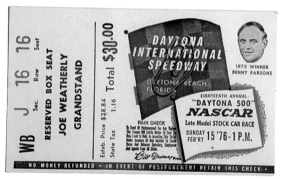

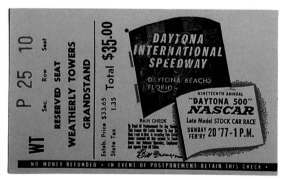

Daytona 500 ticket stubs from 1975, 1976, and 1977 (various grandstands had different color tickets). The previous year's winning driver was shown on the ticket until 1977.

tractive in the sport. Other major sporting events, such as the NFL Super Bowl, have emulated the Indianapolis-style tickets.

For stock car racing collectors, some major NASCAR events have produced interesting and collectible tickets. Ticket stubs are valued for the importance of the event and the artwork on the ticket. A colorful design or a photograph of the previous year's winner often makes a ticket more collectible.

Ticket stubs from the Daytona 500 are the most popular because, as the premier event of the NASCAR season, it is the most significant.

The inaugural Daytona 500 ticket from 1959 is neither colorful nor does it contain any special artwork, but it is very rare and is the most desired ticket stub in stock car racing. The 1960 Daytona 500 ticket had the same rather uninteresting look, but beginning in 1961 the tickets were larger and included the previous year's winner. Like many other tracks, different grandstands at Daytona had different color tickets.

Unfortunately for race fans, the tradition of including the previous year's winner on the Daytona 500 ticket ended in 1977, although the tickets remained similar in design until 1983 when Daytona went to a much smaller ticket size. The twenty-fifth anniversary Daytona ticket in 1983 was appropriately printed in silver, but ticket designs have been disappointing since then.

Daytona tickets from the beach road course era in the 1950s have little appeal from a design

Ticket from the first Daytona 500 in 1959. This is a rare, historic item that few collectors are lucky enough to obtain. The 1960 ticket was similar in size and style. A larger ticket showing the previous year's winner was introduced in 1961.

The 1983 Daytona 500 ticket stub is silver in honor of the speedway's twenty-fifth anniversary. The 1988 ticket is typical of the new computer-generated tickets.

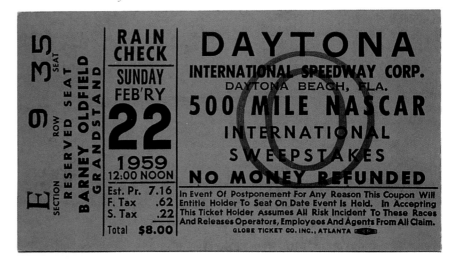

Ticket from the south turn grandstand at the famous Daytona Beach road course from 1954. Memorabilia from the races on the beach is highly sought by collectors.

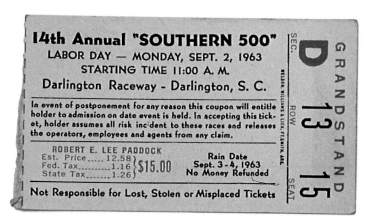

14th Annual "SOUTHERN 500"
LABOR DAY — MONDAY, SEPT. 2, 1963
STARTING TIME 11:00 A.M.
Darlington Raceway - Darlington, S. C.

In event of postponement for any reason this coupon will entitle holder to admission on date event is held. In accepting this ticket, holder assumes all risk incident to these races and releases the operators, employees and agents from any claim.

ROBERT E. LEE PADDOCK
Est. Price ____ 12.58
Fed. Tax ____ 1.16 $15.00
State Tax ____ 1.26

Rain Date
Sept. 3-4, 1963
No Money Refunded

Not Responsible for Lost, Stolen or Misplaced Tickets

GRANDSTAND D
SEC. ROW 13 SEAT 15

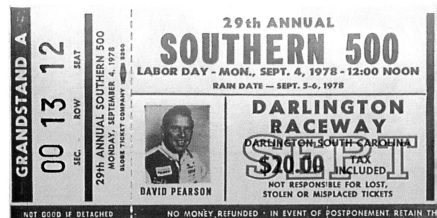

29th ANNUAL SOUTHERN 500
LABOR DAY - MON., SEPT. 4, 1978 - 12:00 NOON
RAIN DATE — SEPT. 5-6, 1978

GRANDSTAND A
SEC. 00 ROW 13 SEAT 12

29th ANNUAL SOUTHERN 500
MONDAY, SEPTEMBER 4, 1978
GLOBE TICKET COMPANY $280

DAVID PEARSON

DARLINGTON RACEWAY
DARLINGTON, SOUTH CAROLINA
$20.00 TAX INCLUDED
SEPT

NOT RESPONSIBLE FOR LOST, STOLEN OR MISPLACED TICKETS

NOT GOOD IF DETACHED · NO MONEY REFUNDED · IN EVENT OF POSTPONEMENT RETAIN TH

DARLINGTON RACEWAY
DARLINGTON, S. C.
NASCAR SANCTIONED
— 7th ANNUAL SOUTHERN "500" —
500 MILE STRICTLY STOCK CAR RACE
$35,000.00 PURSE

LABOR DAY, SEPTEMBER 3, 1956
STARTING TIME 11:00 A. M.

IN EVENT OF POSTPONEMENT FOR ANY REASON THIS COUPON WILL ENTITLE HOLDER TO ADMISSION ON DATE EVENT IS HELD. IN ACCEPTING THIS TICKET HOLDER ASSUMES ALL RISK INCIDENT TO THESE RACES AND RELEASES THE OPERATORS, EMPLOYEES AND AGENTS FROM ANY CLAIM. RAIN DATES: SEPT. 4-5

NO MONEY REFUNDED

ESTAB. PRICE $5.00
FED. TAX .50
STATE TAX .50
TOTAL $6.00

DARLINGTON RACEWAY PROMOTION

GRANDSTAND B
SEC. F ROW 13 SEAT 24

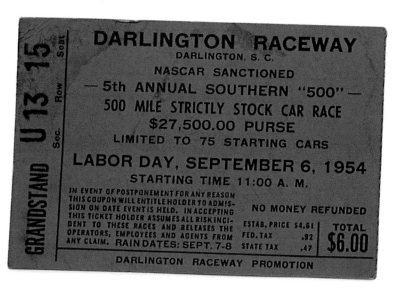

DARLINGTON RACEWAY
DARLINGTON, S. C.
NASCAR SANCTIONED
— 5th ANNUAL SOUTHERN "500" —
500 MILE STRICTLY STOCK CAR RACE
$27,500.00 PURSE
LIMITED TO 75 STARTING CARS

LABOR DAY, SEPTEMBER 6, 1954
STARTING TIME 11:00 A. M.

IN EVENT OF POSTPONEMENT FOR ANY REASON THIS COUPON WILL ENTITLE HOLDER TO ADMISSION ON DATE EVENT IS HELD. IN ACCEPTING THIS TICKET HOLDER ASSUMES ALL RISK INCIDENT TO THESE RACES AND RELEASES THE OPERATORS, EMPLOYEES AND AGENTS FROM ANY CLAIM. RAIN DATES: SEPT. 7-8

NO MONEY REFUNDED

ESTAB. PRICE $4.61
FED. TAX .92
STATE TAX .47
TOTAL $6.00

DARLINGTON RACEWAY PROMOTION

GRANDSTAND U
SEC. ROW 13 SEAT 15

COLVIN GRANDSTAND
EST. PRICE 28.85
TAX 1.15 Total $30.00
1984 SOUTHERN 500
PP 12 8
SEC. ROW SEAT

35th ANNUAL
SOUTHERN 500
SUNDAY
SEPTEMBER 2, 1984
1:00 P.M.

Darlington Raceway

"TOO TOUGH TO TAME"

ROBERT E. LEE PADDOCK
$25.00 1979 SOUTHERN 500
B 4 23
SEC. ROW SEAT

12TH ANNUAL "SOUTHERN 500
— NASCAR SANCTIONED —
LABOR DAY
MONDAY, SEPT. 4, 1961
STARTING TIME 11:00 A. M.
$65,000.00 PURSE
Darlington Raceway — Darlington, S.

In event of postponement for any reason this co will entitle holder to admission on date event is In accepting this ticket, holder assumes all risk inc to these races and releases the operators, emplo and agents from any claim.

Est. Price $8.41
Fed. Tax .74 TOTAL $10.00
State Tax .85

RAIN DAT
SEPT. 5-6, 1
NO MONEY REFU

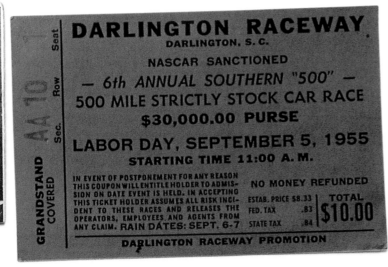

standpoint; however, due to their historical prominence, these tickets have also become quite valuable. The same holds true for Southern 500 ticket stubs from Darlington in the 1950s, and to a lesser degree the World 600 at Charlotte during the 1960s.

Aside from the major Winston Cup races such as the Daytona 500, it is also desirable to collect ticket stubs from races featuring an important milestone, such as Richard Petty's 200th win. When momentous events occur during a relatively minor race, the tickets are of great interest to collectors. A program or ticket stub from Richard Petty or Dale Earnhardt's first Grand National race or win is certainly a collector's item. Few race fans would know these particular race dates unless they checked the history books. So when you find a "regular" old ticket stub, it is a good idea to check what happened at that race; you might be pleasantly surprised.

In recent years, several tracks have improved the quality of their tickets and have created colorful and exciting mementos worth saving. Richard Petty's last race at Atlanta was commemorated with a very attractive ticket. The inaugural Brickyard

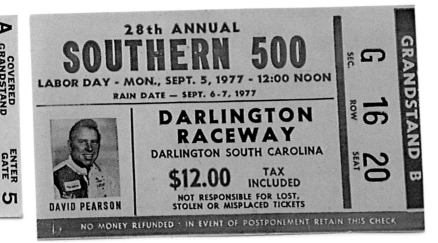

Tickets for the Southern 500 at Darlington Speedway have taken a variety of sizes and designs over the past five decades. For some years, the previous year's winner is shown on the ticket. Darlington has one of the smallest seating capacities of any NASCAR Winston Cup track, making its tickets fewer in number and harder to find.

400 ticket is very collectible. The Winston Cup at Charlotte Motor Speedway features large, colorful commemorative ticket designs. The last Winston Cup race at North Wilkesboro had a special ticket issued for race fans.

Some collectors look for "full" or unused tickets. Although these are tougher to find, they are not necessarily worth more than stubs. In fact, many collectors prefer stubs because they indicate the ticket holder actually attended the race. A surprisingly large number of racing collectors purchased tickets to the inaugural Brickyard 400 and purposely did not use them; consequently, there are many unused tickets from this race.

Condition is very important when collecting tickets. For optimum value, they should not have creases, and the stub should be cleanly separated

at the perforation. Reserved grandstand seats are always worth more than general admission tickets. General admission tickets are usually smaller tickets and do not have the same collectibility as reserved tickets.

Sadly, most tickets are now computer generated with very little artwork or photographs to make them unique to a particular event, resulting

A ticket commemorating both fifty years of racing and the last Winston Cup race held at North Wilkesboro Speedway in 1996. Originally a dirt track, the speedway was not paved until 1957. This North Carolina track was one of the last of the original short tracks that witnessed the birth of major league stock car racing. This pseudo-ticket was bound into the program for the last event and was not an actual admission ticket.

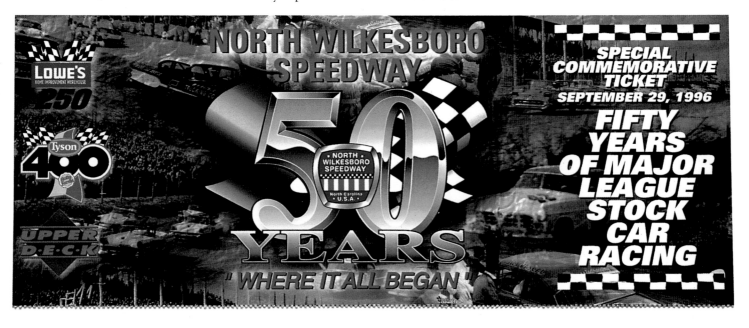

NASCAR credentials during the 1950s were often simply paper tags, such as this competitor permit from Darlington's Southern 500 in 1956. Few of these credentials have survived over the years, making them a challenge to collect.

in a bland appearance. Despite this, ticket stubs are one of the fastest-growing segments of the hobby.

Many ticket stubs are eventually worth much more than the face value of the ticket when it was new!

Credentials

Like a backstage pass to a concert, credentials to a racing event allow access that few fans ever have the chance to experience. Credentials are like a limited-edition ticket, issued to people closely involved with some aspect of the race: media, sponsors, pit crews, track staff, and other VIPs.

Credentials help control access to areas that are generally off limits to the public, including the pits, garage area, press box, and various hospitality areas. They most often take the form of a paper pass, however, buttons, pins, badges, and string tags of virtually every size and shape have been used as credentials.

Many of the NASCAR event credentials have become collectible in recent years. Like tickets or

programs, the age and significance of the race they represent are key factors in determining their value. For example, a credential from the first Daytona 500 in 1959 or Richard Petty's 200th career win at the 1984 Firecracker 400 are more desirable than most other credentials.

In the early days of stock car racing, credentials were often crude in design, sometimes merely a small piece of cardboard with a safety pin to attach it to clothing. With the formation of

A variety of Southern 500 credentials from the 1960s and early 1970s. Darlington's Labor Day weekend classic remains one of NASCAR's most significant events because it occurs at stock car racing's first superspeedway. The numbers on the credentials signify levels of access. Each track uses a different numbering system, which often varies from year to year.

NASCAR, credentials became more standardized.

The Indianapolis Motor Speedway has issued a variety of colorful and beautifully designed credentials for the Indy 500, including the famous metal pit badges, a tradition which began in 1938 and still thrives today.

The Southern 500, stock car racing's premier event in the 1950s, became the first NASCAR Grand National race to produce a metal badge credential. In 1956, the Darlington Raceway created a beautiful bronze badge showing the Plymouth Fury pace car. Individually numbered, the badges had pin-backs for affixing to the wearer's clothing. The following year, Darlington produced another badge for the Southern 500, this time in the shape of a Firestone tire. These two pit badges are considered among the most collectible of all NASCAR race credentials.

For the remainder of the 1950s and early 1960s, Darlington utilized paper credentials, usually with plastic name badges on the top and pin-backs for attaching to clothing.

The Daytona 500 credentials for the inaugural 500 in 1959 were rather plain, although shareholders in the track (International Speedway Corporation) received a special bronze badge in the shape of the speedway logo. The 1960

Above: A Special bronze badge for shareholders in International Speedway Corporation (Daytona International Speedway). The badge was distributed prior to the inaugural Daytona 500 in 1959. Each badge is numbered.

Left: The 1956 Southern 500 metal credential badge depicted the Plymouth Fury pace car. This is one of the few metal pit badges issued for a NASCAR event, making it a very popular collectible. Each badge was individually numbered and included a ribbon. The 1957 Southern 500 credential badge featured a Firestone tire.

Below: A credential and Winston Cup button commemorating the twenty-fifth anniversary of the Daytona 500 in 1983. This was the last year a button was issued along with a Daytona credential. The race was won by Cale Yarborough.

Daytona 500 used plastic-tagged credentials similar to Darlington.

In 1961, a metal pit badge credential sponsored by Autolite Spark Plugs was issued for the Daytona 500. This badge is very rare and considered the most valuable of all Daytona credentials. From 1962 to 1964 Daytona went back to a paper credential with a plastic pin-tag on the top.

Beginning in 1965, Daytona issued a "Daytona International Speedway" metal button with a paper credential. This standard button was used for over two decades, although the button design changed periodically, eventually going to a Winston Cup button. In 1983, for the Speedway's twenty-fifth anniversary, a special silver button was included with the credential. More recently, credentials have

Above left: Credentials from Atlanta International Raceway during the 1960s included colorful buttons, making them very popular among collectors.

Above: A credential and button from the 1981 World 600 at Charlotte Motor Speedway. Credentials issued with buttons are often more valuable, especially if the button is dated. Bobby Allison won this race driving a Buick owned by Harry Ranier.

Above right: A 1964 credential from Martinsville Speedway. Martinsville is one of the oldest NASCAR tracks, opening in 1947.

become smaller in size to fit the plastic credential holders used by all tracks and racing organizations.

Because the Daytona 500 is preceded by more than a week of preliminary events, including the Twin 125s, credentials often were issued for only a given day. There were different styles and formats for each year, depending on the level of access. Daytona 500 credentials and vehicle parking stickers are very difficult to find because they were issued in much fewer numbers than admission tickets.

Although Darlington and Daytona are by far the most popular credentials, probably the most attractive were those issued by Atlanta Motor Speedway throughout the 1960s. Atlanta's credentials were printed on heavy paper and included a colorful, dated button for each particular event. These are quite special compared to other track's credentials.

Other NASCAR tracks such as Martinsville, Bristol, and Charlotte had custom-designed buttons issued with their credentials during the 1960s. Today, most track credentials are somewhat featureless, including garage passes that are often a standard NASCAR credential with the name of the track rubber-stamped on the front. Indianapolis is an exception; it continues to issue very attractive credentials for the Brickyard 400, although it does not produce a metal pit badge similar to those issued for the Indy 500.

Credentials are usually difficult to find in perfect condition, especially those from the early years before protective credential holders were

NASCAR armbands from the 1952 and 1953 seasons. These early versions are seldom found and usually command very high prices when available.

This is an example of the cardboard credential from the 1957 Southern 500 at Darlington that was issued to the timing and scoring staff. Speedy Thompson won the race that year at an average speed of 100 MPH, a new Darlington record.

devised. In addition, few people bothered to save their credentials.

Many tracks and racing organizations are now utilizing "hard cards," a season-long credential and photo identification that resembles a driver's license.

A display of credentials from various tracks is a great conversation piece and showcases an integral aspect of racing history. Credentials are destined to become one of the most popular categories of memorabilia collecting.

NASCAR Armbands

If you look closely at historic stock car racing videos or photographs, you may notice officials wearing armbands. From 1950 through the early 1970s, NASCAR issued armbands to help competitors identify various officials at races.

NASCAR armbands are extremely rare. Even the most dedicated collectors rarely find them. Since armbands were often dated, they were seldom saved because new ones were issued every year. The armbands had various titles such as official, technical inspector, announcer, chief steward, and industry representative.

SCORER

EIGHTH SOUTHERN 500

SOUTHERN

Good for Gate Admission

and

Scoring Stand Area

ONLY

Sped 1970

NASCAR armbands were produced from 1948 through the early 1970s. Since most of them were dated, they were usually discarded when the year ended, making them very hard to find. They were issued for various categories, including pit steward, official, and technical inspector. Armbands were not credentials, but they allowed officials to be easily identified.

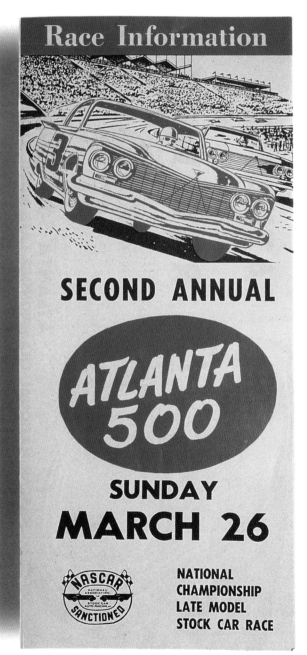

Large patches for jackets were also issued by NASCAR. These look similar to armbands, and were often attached to the striped NASCAR "referee jackets" worn in the 1950s.

Ticket Brochures

Every major track that hosted a Winston Cup event printed ticket brochures, which were distributed at most NASCAR events and also mailed to fans who purchased tickets the prior year. Ticket brochures were printed in a standard 3 ½-by-8 ½-inch size and were usually full color. The ticket brochures were primarily issued from the late 1950s to the mid-1980s. Although ticket order brochures are still printed in various formats by some tracks, they became less necessary as tracks

Left: A ticket brochure from the 1961 Atlanta 500. The race was won by a relatively obscure driver named Bob Burdick, who started only fifteen races during his entire career. This was Burdick's only NASCAR Grand National victory.

Right: The 1968 Daytona 500 ticket brochure. The artwork on the cover shows drivers Fireball Roberts, Mario Andretti, Richard Petty, and Fred Lorenzen. Andretti was the defending Daytona 500 champion.

Far right: As the defending champion, Richard Petty was featured on the cover of the 1965 Daytona 500 ticket brochure.

FEB. 25, 1968 — 12:30 P.M.

DAYTONA 500

SCHEDULE OF EVENTS
AND ORDER BLANK

DAYTONA USA

1962
"FIREBALL" ROBERTS

1967
MARIO ANDRETTI

1964, 1966
RICHARD PETTY

1965
FRED LORENZEN

DATE: FEB. 14, 1965   TIME: 12:30 P.M.

DAYTONA 500

1965 SCHEDULE OF EVENTS

World's Fastest 500 Mile Race

A 1957 NASCAR driver's pin. These pins were sent to drivers when their annual memberships were renewed. The pins were not credentials and were not required to be worn during a race.

A NASCAR member pin for the 1956 season and driver pin for the 1952 season. Driver pins are more difficult to find than member pins, which were produced in much greater numbers for race fans. These pins are quite small and have screw posts on the back for attaching to clothing.

A 1965 NASCAR pin, the last year a dated pin was issued by NASCAR.

went to computer renewal systems and because most Winston Cup races are sold out several months prior to the event.

Ticket brochures are very popular among specialized collectors, and complement ticket stub and program collections.

NASCAR Membership Pins

NASCAR membership pins are very popular collectibles. They date back to the organization's very first season in 1948. However, NASCAR was far from the first to issue such pins. The first memberships pins were issued by the American Automobile Association (AAA). AAA was the major racing organization in the United States up until 1955, and every year it produced dated pins for drivers, car owners, and mechanics (also known then as "mechanicians"). These pins featured beautiful designs and were usually the size of a dime or smaller. Extremely rare, AAA pins from the 1930s and earlier have become very valuable.

When NASCAR began its first full season in 1948, the sanctioning organization followed the

A variety of NASCAR membership pins. The style, size, and color has changed through the years, however, it is not known how many were produced or why some years have different categories—driver, mechanic, owner, member— and others don't.

examples of other racing groups by issuing four different membership pins: driver, car owner, member, and mechanic. These pins and the similar tie clasps from NASCAR's first season are quite rare. Unfortunately, they have also been reproduced without authorization, and the copies are difficult to tell from the originals.

NASCAR continued to issue at least one dated pin every year through 1965, changing the size, style, color, and logo over the years. Many membership pins from the early 1950s are scarce and have steadily increased in value. NASCAR has also issued various membership cards since 1949, usually called the "Annual License." They most often measure 4 by 2 $\frac{1}{4}$ inches and have the date on the cover, opening up to the member's information on the inside (there is both a non-competitive and a competitor version).

Sports Illustrated

FEBRUARY 28, 1977 ONE DOLLAR

GREAT DAY AT DAYTONA

Cale Yarborough wins the 500

CHAPTER 4

Books, Magazines, Yearbooks & Other Publications

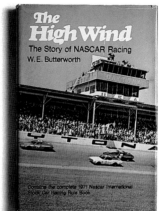

Before television and VCRs, the only way stock car racing fans could follow the cars and stars of NASCAR racing was through books and magazines. They were the next best thing to being there in person, since newspapers seldom covered stock car racing until only a few years ago.

Over the years there have been hundreds of publications on racing, although only a relatively small number have been devoted exclusively to stock car racing. For fans and historians, many of these publications have become valued memorabilia, not only for their monetary worth, but also for their entertainment and research value.

Books

For racing collectors, the number of classic stock car books is certainly limited when compared to other forms of racing. After all, stock car racing has not been around that long. While a plethora of new books have come out over the past few years, collectors are hard pressed to find copies of titles published before 1980.

The High Wind: The Story of NASCAR Racing by W. E. Butterworth, published in 1971, was one of the first books specifically on NASCAR racing.

Above: Very few books were published on stock car racing until the early 1970s. The High Wind was one of the first to describe NASCAR's colorful stars and fast-growing popularity.

Opposite: Issues of Sports Illustrated with cover stories on stock car racing, such as this 1977 issue featuring the Daytona 500, are popular among collectors. This race was the second of Cale Yarborough's four Daytona 500 wins.

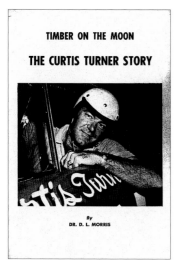

TIMBER ON THE MOON

THE CURTIS TURNER STORY

By
DR. D. L. MORRIS

Published the same year was one of the most entertaining books, *The World's Number One, Flat Out, All Time Great Stock Car Racing Book* by Jerry Bledsoe.

By the mid-1970s several books were published on NASCAR racing, including Hal Higdon's *Showdown at Daytona*, which followed his *Finding the Groove*. Bill Libby's *Heroes of Stock Car Racing*, and Frank Orr's *Great Moments in Stock Car Racing* are other early works on stock car racing.

Most stock car racing books have been about particular drivers. Not surprising, Richard Petty has been the subject of several books, including an autobiography with Bill Neely, *Grand National*, published in 1971, and *King of the Road* published in 1977. David Pearson was featured in *21 Forever* by Jim Hunter. The Wood Brothers, Cale Yarborough, Neil Bonnett, and Bobby Allison, among others, have all been the subject of books.

One of the rarest of all stock car racing books is *Timber on the Moon: The Curtis Turner Story*, published in 1966. This small paperback is highly coveted by collectors of stock car racing memorabilia and is one of the first to feature a NASCAR star.

Most out-of-print stock car racing books are quite common and can be found in used bookstores. They are most valuable if the dust jacket is in excellent condition.

Left: Timber on the Moon *is considered the rarest of all stock car racing books. Published in 1966, the paperback is about Curtis Turner, winner of seventeen NASCAR Grand National races during his career. Turner was a flamboyant driver known for hard driving and equally hard living. He was killed in a plane crash in 1970.*

Opposite: 1966 was the inaugural year for Stock Car Racing *magazine, and this June issue was the first to cover Daytona Speed Weeks. Issues from the 1960s and the 1970s are particularly popular with collectors since no other magazine covered NASCAR at that time.* Stock Car Racing *thrives today as a leading monthly racing magazine.*

There have also been books published on specific tracks, including six different books on Daytona, and one each on Darlington and Talladega. Jim Hunter's *A History of Darlington Raceway*, published in 1960, was one of the earliest books on a particular track. Bill Tuthill's *Speed on Sand* was a small but very informative book describing the early days of racing at Daytona.

Greg Fielden's five-volume history of NASCAR Grand National/Winston Cup racing, *40 Years of Stock Car Racing*, is one of the best research sources a NASCAR collector can own. Fielden has also published a book on the NASCAR Convertible Division, *Rumblin' Ragtops*.

Magazines

Stock Car Racing is by far the most widely collected magazine on the sport. It first appeared in 1966, and many of the issues published prior to 1970 are quite scarce. *Stock Car Racing* is one of the best sources of information on the sport.

Grand National Scene (now titled *NASCAR Winston Cup Scene*) was a popular weekly tabloid and is also an excellent source of information, but not as popular among collectors as its sister publication, *Grand National Illustrated* (now known as *NASCAR*

STOCK CAR RACING

STOCK CAR

·the racing fan's magazine·

JUNE
SIXTY CENTS

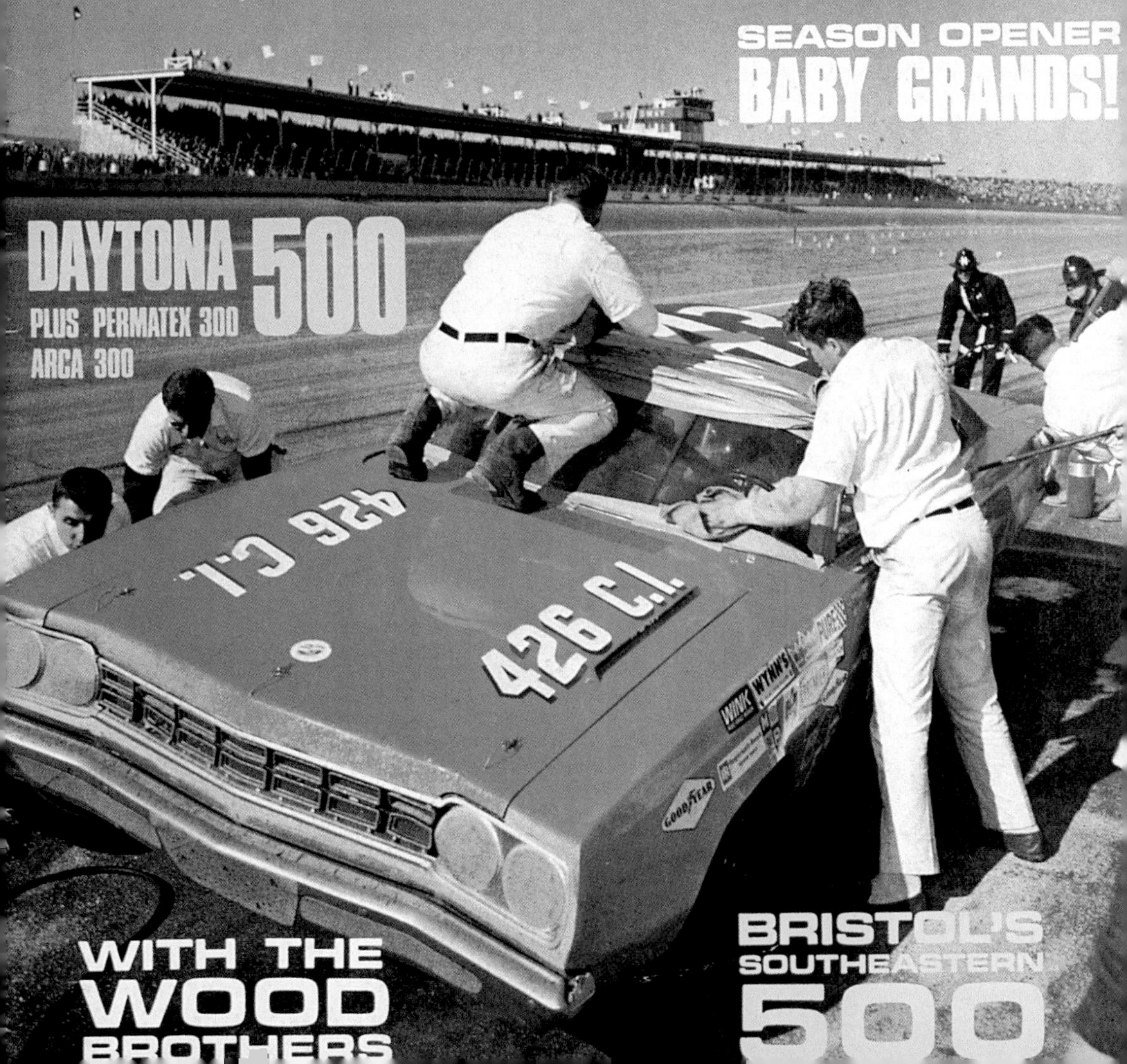

SEASON OPENER
BABY GRANDS!

DAYTONA **500**
PLUS PERMATEX 300
ARCA 300

426 C.I.

426 C.I.

WITH THE
WOOD
BROTHERS

BRISTOL'S
SOUTHEASTERN
500

Grand
National

THE AUTOBIOGRAPHY OF RICHARD PETTY

as told to Bill Neely

Left: Several books have been published on Richard Petty, the king of NASCAR racing with 200 career victories. His early 1970s autobiography, Grand National, *was one of the first widely circulated stock car racing books.*

Below: David Pearson, NASCAR's second all-time winningest driver, was the subject of this book that followed Petty's. The title 21 Forever *refers to his car's racing number.*

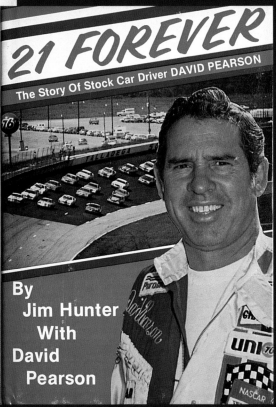

21 FOREVER
The Story Of Stock Car Driver DAVID PEARSON

By
Jim Hunter
With
David
Pearson

Right: Racing Pictorial *covered NASCAR racing in the 1960s and 1970s. Its extensive use of colorful photography make it a prized collectible and great reference source.* Racing Pictorial *also produced special publications on NASCAR, such as this* Grand National Stars and Cars, *as well as booklets on race cars. Shown on the cover is 1973 Grand National champion Benny Parsons with L. G. DeWitt, president of North Carolina Motor Speedway in Rockingham.*

Below right: Grand National Illustrated *(now* NASCAR Winston Cup Illustrated*) is a stock car racing magazine that is destined to be a collectible due to its extensive coverage of the stars of the NASCAR circuit as well as NASCAR history. This 1984 issue has Harry Hyde on the cover, crew chief for Geoff Bodine at the time.*

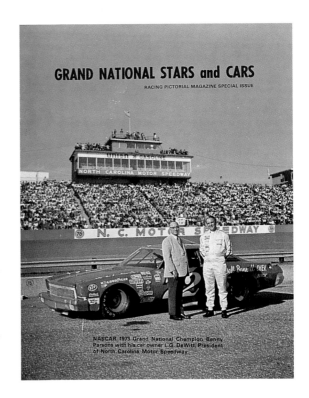

Winston Cup Illustrated*), a glossy monthly magazine.

Circle Track & Highway magazine, which lasted only a few years, is also quite popular among collectors. (It has no relation to the current magazine called *Circle Track.*)

Of course, there are many other periodicals that cover stock car racing, but few are widely collected. For research, *National Speed Sport News* (1934–present) and *Speed Age* (1947–1959) are probably the two best resources on early stock car racing history.

The official *NASCAR Newsletter* has been published in various formats since 1952. Usually issued on a weekly basis during the racing season, the newsletter is an excellent resource. Issues from the 1950s and 1960s are scarce and their values seem to be steadily climbing as collectors and historians discover their usefulness as a research tool.

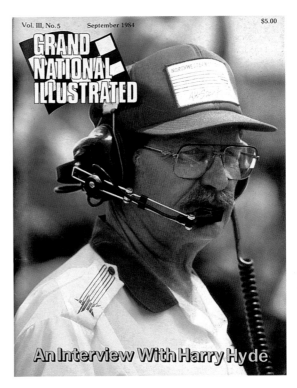

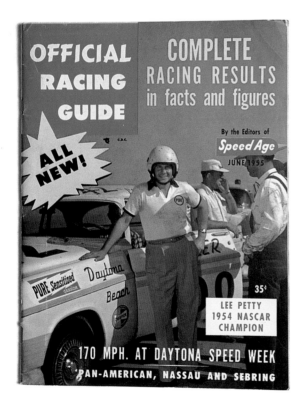

Yearbooks

Yearbooks, or annuals, have been quite popular among racing collectors. Daytona Speed Week yearbooks have been produced since 1984 in various formats (the 1985 edition is very rare). The NASCAR yearbook and the hard-cover Winston Cup yearbook are two popular books published every year. (Retrospective editions are now being published for earlier years, such as 1979.)

The only NASCAR race other than the Daytona 500 that has an annual published for it is the Brickyard 400. Two different publishers offer a yearbook for that event. Of course, there are other sanctioning body publications issued by the Automobile Racing Club of America (ARCA), American Speed Association (ASA), and various regional organizations.

The oldest publication known to exist on stock car racing is the *1941 Stock Car Racing Record Book*, which covered the major events of that year. Its origin is unknown as it was not produced by any particular organization. It is very rare. NASCAR

Left: During the 1950s, a monthly magazine called Speed Age *covered stock car racing extensively. They also issued an annual racing guide.*

Opposite: The first NASCAR yearbook was published in 1950 and covered the 1949 season. The large-format book is one of the most sought after of all stock car racing publications. NASCAR yearbooks have been issued every year except 1956.

1950
NASCAR
Yearbook

A 1954 NASCAR Yearbook.

The 1957 NASCAR press guide was a similar size and format used by most professional sports teams at that time. This edition is the most difficult to find because of its limited distribution.

The 1958 NASCAR Yearbook pictured the champions of the previous season on the cover, including Grand National Champion Buck Baker, Convertible Champion Bob Welborn, Short Track Champion Jim Reed, Sportsman Champion Ned Jarrett, and Modified Champion Ken Marriott.

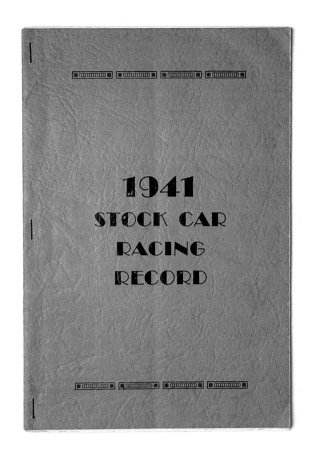

Right: The earliest stock car racing yearbook known to exist was published in 1941, six years before the formation of NASCAR. It only gives results from various events, mainly in the South, and does not contain photographs.

yearbooks are perhaps the most worthwhile pieces of memorabilia available to collectors, filled with facts and figures on all of NASCAR's divisions.

The first NASCAR yearbook was published in 1950 and covered the 1949 season (all subsequent NASCAR yearbooks have been dated in this manner).

While modern NASCAR yearbooks are distributed by the tens of thousands to bookstores and newsstands all over the country, the early NASCAR yearbooks were available only by mail, and most of the early editions are quite difficult to find.

The first three NASCAR yearbooks were a large 9-by-12-inch format and are considered among the finest yearbooks ever published by a sanctioning organization. They were produced for NASCAR by Houston Lawing, who also produced programs for Darlington Raceway and would later join Daytona International Speedway.

The yearbooks went to a smaller booklet-size format for 1953 and 1954, then moved to a standard magazine size in 1955. There was no yearbook produced in 1956.

Beginning in 1957, the NASCAR yearbooks, often titled *Record Book for Press, Radio and Television,* also served as the organization's media guide. They went to the smaller 4-by-8-inch shirt-pocket-size format used by most professional sports teams. For the next several years, the NASCAR yearbooks were made available primarily to NASCAR members, sports writers, and broadcasters, with only a small number offered to race fans.

In 1972, the NASCAR yearbooks were printed in an even smaller size with a perfect binding. These editions contain comprehensive results and race records, making them convenient resources. The 1973 edition commemorated NASCAR's silver anniversary with the twenty-fifth anniversary logo on the front and was produced with rounded corners. The small booklet-size format continued through the 1982 edition.

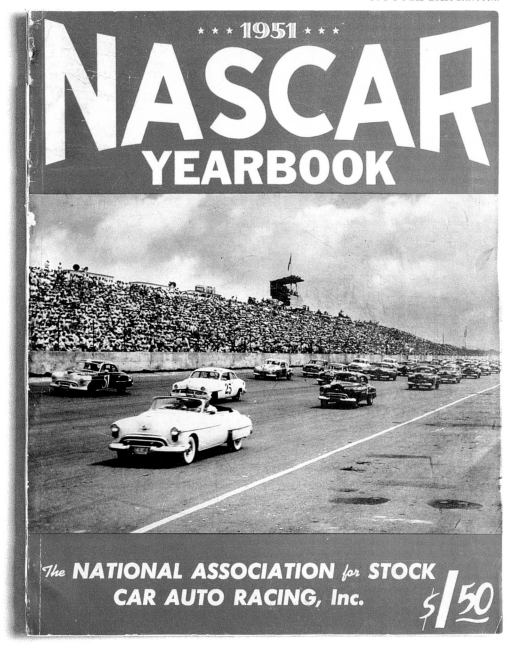

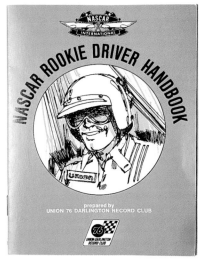

Above: A rare NASCAR Rookie Driver Handbook from the early 1970s. Printed in small quantities, these handbooks are difficult to find. The booklet gave rookies tips on how to adjust to the NASCAR circuit and a basic overview of rules and procedures.

Right: The 1955 NASCAR Yearbook was the first edition produced in the standard magazine-size format. The cover shows the 1954 champions from the major NASCAR divisions, including Grand National Champion Lee Petty. Also shown are Short Track Champion Jim Reed, Modified Champion Jack Choquette, and Sportsman Champion Danny Graves. For reasons that are now unknown, there was no NASCAR yearbook published in 1956.

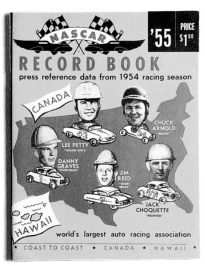

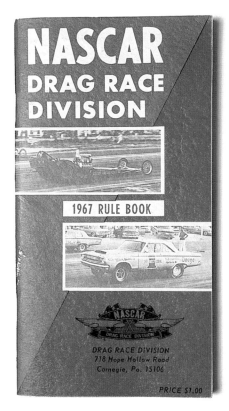

Many race fans don't know that NASCAR sanctioned drag racing during the mid 1960s. This 1967 rule book is very rare. NASCAR has also dabbled in sports car racing, Indy car racing, and midget racing.

In the late 1960s, long before calculators and laptop computers, NASCAR produced this timing "Computer-Pak". It included charts for figuring average speed and other statistics.

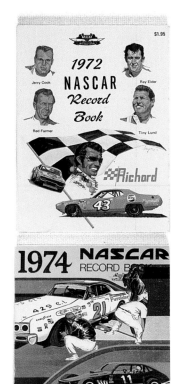

Left: During the 1970s, NASCAR yearbooks went to a smaller format. A special twenty-fifth anniversary logo was used on the cover of the 1973 edition.

Opposite: During the 1960s NASCAR yearbooks (referred to as record books "for press, radio and television") were issued primarily for the media. Few were distributed to race fans. The covers show the previous year's champions from the major NASCAR divisions, with the Grand National winner given the most prominent position.

Below: The NASCAR Newsletter was first published in 1952. This issue from 1954 shows a drawing of the proposed Daytona International Speedway, which became a reality five years later. The newsletters were usually eight to sixteen pages and included results and point standings, making them an excellent reference for historians.

NASCAR began issuing separate media guides for Winston Cup, Grand National, and Winston West beginning in 1983, going back to a 4-by-9-inch size.

As NASCAR's popularity began reaching record levels in 1986, the organization started producing a magazine-size yearbook geared primarily to race fans, while continuing separate publications strictly for the media. This format of the NASCAR yearbook continues today.

Yearbooks are an important part of NASCAR's heritage, especially for difficult-to-find information on NASCAR results, point standings, and other historical statistics from the early years. Hobbyists should consider making them a key part of their collection.

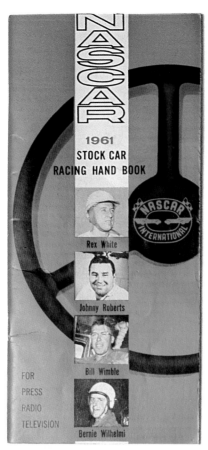

NASCAR
1961
STOCK CAR
RACING HAND BOOK

Rex White

Johnny Roberts

Bill Wimble

Bernie Wilhelmi

FOR
PRESS
RADIO
TELEVISION

NASCAR
1962
STOCK CAR
RACING RECORD BOOK

NED JARRETT

BILL WIMBLE

DICK NEPHEW

JOHNNY ROBERTS

FOR PRESS ·
RADIO · TELEVISION

NASCAR
STOCK CAR
RACING RECORD BOOK
1963

JOE WEATHERLY

RENE CHARLAND

EDDIE CROUSE

FOR PRESS · RADIO ·
TELEVISION

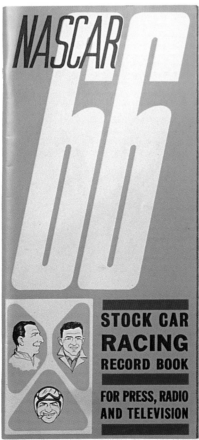

NASCAR
66

STOCK CAR
RACING
RECORD BOOK

FOR PRESS, RADIO
AND TELEVISION

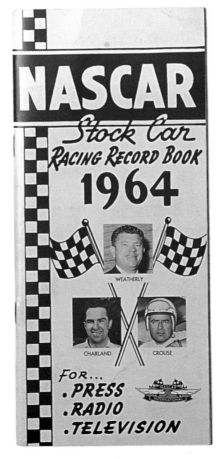

NASCAR
Stock Car
RACING RECORD BOOK
1964

WEATHERLY

CHARLAND

CROUSE

FOR...
· PRESS
· RADIO
· TELEVISION

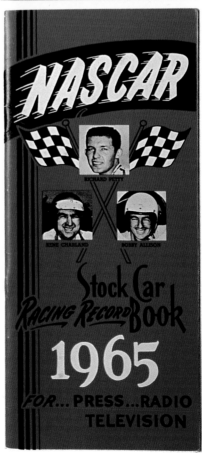

NASCAR

RICHARD PETTY

RENE CHARLAND

BOBBY ALLISON

Stock Car
Racing Record Book
1965

FOR... PRESS ...RADIO
TELEVISION

NASCAR Rule Books

NASCAR rule books are popular for collectors, historians, and race car restoration specialists. While they are not as attractive from a visual standpoint as other NASCAR publications, they are an integral part of NASCAR's development and an official way to document the evolution of the sport from the "strictly stock" automobiles of the early 1950s to the high-tech, ultra-competitive brand of racing on the Winston Cup circuit today.

Rule books have always been printed in relatively small quantities because they are intended to be used by competitors. And when a new edition came out, the previous year's editions were often discarded. Today, new rule books are available only to race teams. It is nearly impossible for race fans to obtain copies. For this reason, modern NASCAR Winston Cup rule books are destined to become as collectible as the older ones.

The first rule book, which appeared in NASCAR's 1948 inaugural season, was only four pages in length. Today, NASCAR rule books number in the hundreds of pages with technical updates issued throughout the season.

Virtually all NASCAR rule books up to 1972 were pocket-size (4 by 6 inches) and had rather plain covers with the organization's logo and the date. As NASCAR racing became more complex, rule books were printed in a larger 4-by-9-inch format to accommodate the many rules and regu-

lations. Since 1985 the distribution of rule books has been tightly controlled.

NASCAR Award's Banquet Programs

NASCAR's season-ending award's banquet, now held in New York City, has become a social event second to none in the world of racing. The glamorous black-tie affair attracts the who's who of racing and honors the year's champions in an elegant setting. The origins of the NASCAR banquet, however, are quite humble. For over thirty years, the banquet was held at various hotels in Daytona Beach. During the 1950s, these events were relatively small and informal.

A program has been printed for the NASCAR banquet since the first year-end banquet in 1948. It has evolved from a four-page booklet listing the menu to a more elaborate program with photographs of the various champions and the point standings for all NASCAR divisions. These NASCAR banquet programs are very popular but quite difficult to find, especially those prior to 1973.

Above left: NASCAR rule books, such as these from the early 1950s, are becoming very popular among memorabilia collectors and stock car restoration specialists. They are the NASCAR "bible" for race teams, giving complete details regarding rules and technical specifications for race car preparation.

10TH ANNUAL

FEBRUARY – EIGHTEENTH
NINETEEN – FIFTY – NINE

NASCAR
NATIONAL ASSOCIATION FOR STOCK CAR AUTO RACING, INC.
INTERNATIONAL

PRINCESS ISSENA HOTEL
DAYTONA BEACH, FLORIDA

Victory Dinner

HONORING AUTO RACING'S CHAMPIONS

Menu

"PURE PREMIUM" SHRIMP COCKTAIL
"PEDRICK" RELISHES
"CHAMPION" FLORIDA SALAD

"GRAND NATIONAL" TURKEY
"GREY ROCK" DRESSING
"CONVERTIBLE" CANDIED YAMS
"FIRESTONE" HARICOT VERT
"GOODYEAR" HOT ROLLS

"PAUL WHITEMAN'S" APPLE PIE
"PERFECT CIRCLE'S" CHEESE
"TOM McCAHILL'S" COFFEE

SPORTSMEN'S COCKTAILS — 6:15 TO 7:00 P. M.

23rd Annual

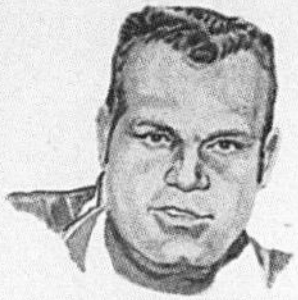

JERRY COOK

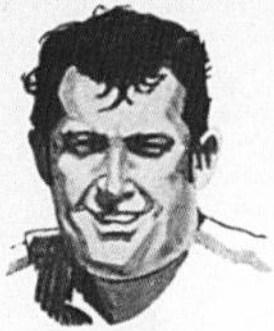

RAY ELDER

NASCAR INTERNATIONAL

Awards, Victory Dinner

Daytona Beach, Florida

RED FARMER

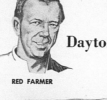

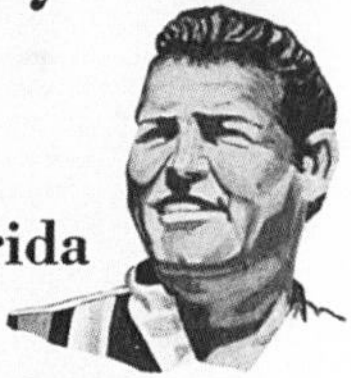

TINY LUND

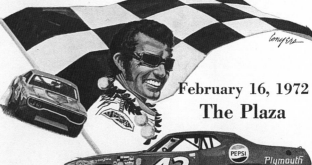

February 16, 1972
The Plaza

Bobby Isaac - Catawaba, N
NASCAR Grand National

David Pearson - Spartanburg, S. C.
NASCAR Grand National

January

1970

	TH	FR	SA	SU	MO	TU	WE	TH	FR	SA	SU	MO	TU	WE	TH	FR	SA
	1	2	3	4	5	6	7	8	9	10	11	12	13	14	15	16	17
				18	19	20	21	22	23	24	25	26	27	28	29	30	31

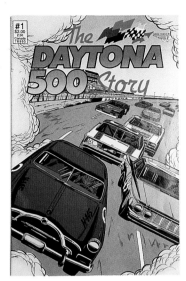

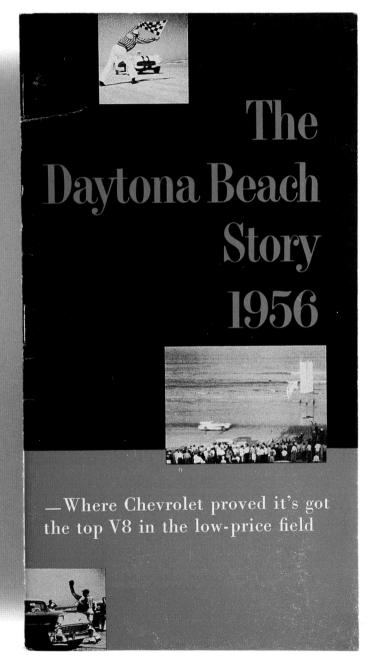

Miscellaneous Publications

Over the first five decades of stock car racing, there were numerous other special publications. Among them are calendars, comic books, press guides, and a variety of booklets produced by sponsors and manufacturers. Examples of several of these publications are shown in this chapter. For collectors, the older the better seems to be the best rule of thumb, because any stock car racing publication featuring NASCAR from the 1950s through the late 1970s is very collectible.

Press kits and other race team publications intended for distribution to the media are popular among collectors. Often in the form of a folder, they contain interesting photographs and information. While press kits have been around since the 1950s, it was not until the early 1970s that they were utilized on a large scale by virtually every NASCAR team. They have now become very

Left: This booklet by Chevrolet was issued to advertise its success at the 1956 NASCAR performance trials on Daytona Beach. These events were a preliminary to the annual Speed Week classics.

Press kits for stock car racing teams appeared in the 1960s and became more elaborate as corporate involvement in stock car racing grew. Originally rather modest, they have evolved into colorful and intricate presentations. The spiral-bound Purolator Media Guide was issued for David Pearson's 1976 campaign on the Winston Cup circuit. Darrell Waltrip's Gatorade press kit is from 1978, when the brash young driver was just attaining superstar status. Janet Guthrie's rare Kelley Girl Racing Team press kit has historical importance as she was the first female driver to compete in the Daytona 500.

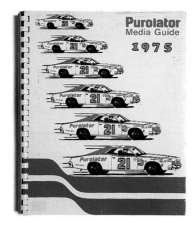

Press kits of superstar NASCAR drivers before they became superstars are popular among collectors. The press kits of Dale Earnhardt, Bill Elliott, and Jeff Gordon were produced before they became household names. Press kits contain publicity photographs, driver biographies, background information on the team and its sponsors, and other information needed by reporters covering the race. Since they are intended to be used exclusively by the media and are not a collectible for race fans, it is considered unethical for memorabilia collectors to buy, sell, or trade current press kits.

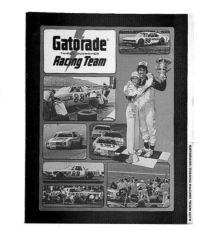

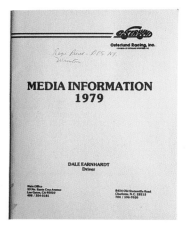

DAYTONA BEACH MORNING JOURNAL

Mystery
WNDB - am - fm —
Another adventure
with The Falcon at
8 p.m.

Open Forum
PAGE 9 — A talk about
"a sort of lost fron-
tier."

VOL. XXX—NO. 45   DAYTONA BEACH, FLORIDA, MONDAY, FEBRUARY 22, 1954   ★   PRICE FIVE CENTS

TIM FLOCK WINS IT

— Skidding and jockeying for position, racers jam their cars through the North Turn.

Sets New Record Of 90.40 M.P.H. In '54 Olds; Lee Petty Second

By BERNARD KAHN
News-Journal Sports Editor

The weather was perfect and Julius Timothy Flock's driving skill was the same yesterday afternoon at the scenic beach n' road track.

The 29 year old father of five established a new speed record in winning the NASCAR 160 mile Grand National Circuit race for new model stock American automobiles.

Under the gaze of a hot tropical sun and an estimated 27,000 spectators, the largest crowd in local history, Flock drove a 1954 Oldsmobile 88 two door sedan to victory at an average speed of 90.40 mph.

The tall, handsome professional race driver from Atlanta finished his Sunday auto ride in one hour, 46 minutes and 11 seconds. Trailing Tim at the finish line by one minute and 28 seconds was 39 year old Lee Petty of Randleman, N.C. behind the wheel of a 1954 Chrysler New Yorker coupe.

Flock surpassed the former record of 89.50 mph which Bill Blair of High Point, N.C., set here last year in a 1953 Olds. Blair piloted a '54 Olds yesterday and came in sixth.

Victory brought Flock first prize money of $1,700, which will help him to buy baby a new pair of shoes. The fifth li'l Flock was born just a week ago at Atlanta. The total purse was only $8,800.

THE NATION

Army Sec'y., McCarthy

AUTO RACING

Win Ends 5 Year Blank

---

elaborate and are in demand by collectors. It is important for collectors to understand that press kits are intended for use by the media and it is considered unethical for a collector to obtain a current one. Only when a press kit is obsolete should race fans and collectors have access to them. (Most show promoters do not allow the sale of press kits at their event unless they are at least five years old.)

Newspapers covering the Daytona Speed Weeks are a popular collectible. In 1959, the *Daytona Beach*

Newspapers covering the NASCAR races on the sands of Daytona Beach during the 1950s are quite scarce. This edition describes Tim Flock's win in 1955.

Journal issued a special souvenir edition for the opening of the new Daytona International Speedway. Every year since then a special Speed Weeks edition has been published. Those editions, plus the newspaper printed the day after the Daytona 500, are now highly desired by collectors.

CHAPTER 5

Toys & Models

The largest and fastest-growing segment of the racing collectibles hobby is diecast cars. In just a few years, this new segment of the NASCAR collectibles hobby has attracted tens of thousands of new collectors.

While some veteran collectors of racing memorabilia regard diecast cars as nothing more than mass-produced souvenirs with no historical significance, they have unquestionably found acceptance among mainstream NASCAR fans.

Diecast

For the most part, diecast cars have replaced plastic model kits on store shelves. Diecast cars offer ease of display and a variety of colorful packaging that many other types of collectibles do not have. Most important, they create in miniature the cars that race fans so readily identify with on the NASCAR circuit.

Diecast toys have been around for many years, but it wasn't until the mid-1980s that they developed into a major segment of NASCAR collecting. Since then, there has been a flurry of new diecast products in a variety of scales.

Racing Champions is a name synonymous with diecast collecting, issuing thousands of cars since

Above: Among the first $^1/_{64}$-scale NASCAR diecast toys was this Dale Earnhardt Wrangler T-Bird issued in 1983 (Earnhardt drove for the Bud Moore team, winning two races that season). Diecast toys are far more valuable if left in the original packaging.

Opposite: An early 1970s Richard Petty Plymouth Superbird plastic model kit by Jo-Han. Models are collectible in part due to their packaging, and this model kit is one of the most attractive. Petty's Plymouth carried him to eighteen wins in 1970 and twenty-one wins the following year.

1989, most in $\frac{1}{64}$ scale. Some of the early issues are scarce and have become quite collectible. A variety of scales are now available from several different manufacturers, with the $\frac{1}{24}$ issue becoming the standard of the hobby.

ERTL was among the first to manufacture NASCAR diecast cars, while Action, Hot Wheels, Matchbox, RCCA, and Revell are just a few of the other brand names most commonly associated with the diecast hobby. Even companies such as the Franklin Mint have entered the market.

Like other forms of toy and model collecting, to appreciate in value, diecast toys should be left in their original packaging. However, NASCAR fans should be skeptical regarding estimated values in printed price guides. Many of the so-called experts who supposedly help set market values have been found to have other motives, such as being major dealers in such products. Most diecast cars have been mass-produced, so collectors should be wary of any claims of a limited edition.

One diecast manufacturer has formulated a unique approach to collecting diecast race cars.

This Darrell Waltrip $\frac{1}{24}$ toy car was one of the first diecast toys to hit the NASCAR market. Along with attractive packaging, it was produced in relatively small quantities compared to today's mass-produced diecast toys. It is one of the few Waltrip collectibles that depicts the Pepsi Challenger paint scheme used during the 1983 season, when he finished second in the Winston Cup standings.

Racing Collectables Club of America (RCCA) offers a variety of diecast cars that are sold only to members. This ensures controlled quantities and distribution. The RCCA diecasts are among the best and they offer a wide variety of cars. Their Elite series features some of the most realistic diecast cars in the hobby.

Sponsors and tracks have utilized diecast NASCAR cars as an important marketing tool, and during a typical Winston Cup season, well over one thousand limited edition diecast cars

The Franklin Mint entered the NASCAR collectibles market with this detailed 1/24-scale Richard Petty STP stock car. Nowhere on the car or in any of the advertising is the car's manufacturer mentioned.

are issued, many with special one-race paint schemes or commemorative packaging. Production runs range from less than a thousand into the tens of thousands.

Matchbox NASCAR team transporters from 1989 are among the most sought after of all diecast toys. Shown at left are haulers for Cale Yarborough's Hardees team, Neil Bonnett's Citgo team, and Dale Earnhardt's Goodwrench Racing Team. The Goodwrench hauler is even more valuable if Earnhardt's signature is found on the cab (these were withdrawn from the market for legal reasons).

Nostalgic diecasts depicting stock car racing stars of the past have been issued in recent years. Shown at left is an ERTL diecast modified stock car driven by Cotton Owens early in his career.

This ERTL NASCAR set features the 1983 Daytona 500 25th Anniversary pace car.

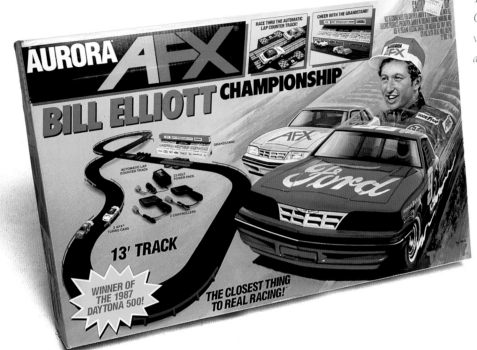

This Bill Elliott slot car set was issued in 1987. His Coors Thunderbird dominated NASCAR at that time, winning nineteen races from 1985 to 1987. The box art shows the car's "Coors" lettering replaced by "Ford".

This 1973 NASCAR Grand National slot car game featured superstars Richard Petty and Bobby Allison. They battled fiercely for the 1972 championship, winning eighteen races between them with Petty coming out on top. This rare set is very valuable, especially when complete.

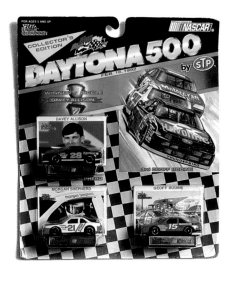

Above: Special packaging that features a particular event, such as this Racing Champions issue for the 1992 Daytona 500, is among the many clever types of packaging utilized to sell diecast cars to collectors.

Above left: Pace cars such as this produced for the inaugural 1994 Brickyard 400 are yet another segment of the diecast hobby. Like many recent limited edition diecast toys, the packaging indicates the total number produced of this edition.

Left: Collecting cars with special one-time paint schemes for specific races is a large part of the diecast hobby. Dale Earnhardt started the trend at the 1995 Winston Select when his tradition-ally black Monte Carlo was painted silver to commemorate twenty-five years of R. J. Reynolds sponsorship. Action Performance created this model for its Racing Collectables Club of America.

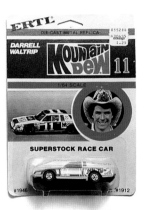

These ¹/₆₄-scale diecast cars were among the early editions that started the diecast craze that has swept the NASCAR collectible hobby. They are very collectible, especially if still in their original packaging. Shown above are Tim Richmond's Folgers car and Darrell Waltrip's Mountain Dew car, both from the early 1980s. Waltrip was at the top of his career at this time, winning the Winston Cup title in 1981, 1982, and 1985. The brash young Richmond was just becoming a superstar when complications from AIDS forced his retirement. He died in 1989.

Novelty diecast products have appeared on the market as well. Haulers, tool carts, airplanes, trucks, and banks—all with NASCAR themes—are available to collectors. Each year hundreds of new diecast cars come on the market, updated with the new livery for NASCAR teams for the upcoming season. In addition, many diecast cars have been produced featuring vintage stock cars of the past. The diecast market has been flooded in recent years and there appears to be no end in sight for this segment of the hobby.

Since most NASCAR collectors specialize in diecasts of their favorite driver, cars of the most popular drivers are actually the most common, while diecast issues of less popular drivers are actually the most collectible.

Models

Model building has been a favorite pastime for many generations. Model ships, airplanes, and cars are a part of Americana, a hobby that kids and adults both enjoy.

Plastic model kits rapidly grew in popularity during the late 1950s and throughout the 1960s. Nearly every make and model of car has found its way onto the shelves of the local hobby shop or

A sticker advertising his Daytona 500 win in 1992 was added to this Davey Allison T-Bird model. Sadly, Allison was killed in a helicopter crash at Talladega in 1993.

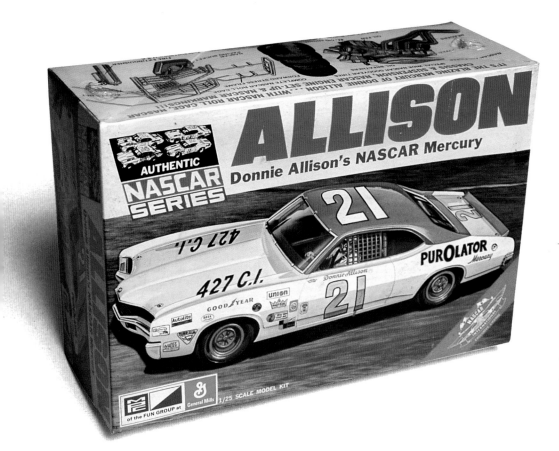

The MPC models of the early 1970s were the first to feature NASCAR cars and drivers. They are also among the first products to be officially licensed by NASCAR. Left: The Wood Brothers' Mercury driven by Donnie Allison. From his thirteen starts in the 1971 season, Allison won one race and had eight top ten finishes. Below left: Bobby Isaac won thirty-seven NASCAR races in his career and the 1970 points championship. He died in 1977 of a heart attack after driving in a short track race. Below right: This Roger Penske-prepared AMC Matador model kit is very rare. In 1975 Bobby Allison won three races and posted ten top-five finishes in 19 starts.

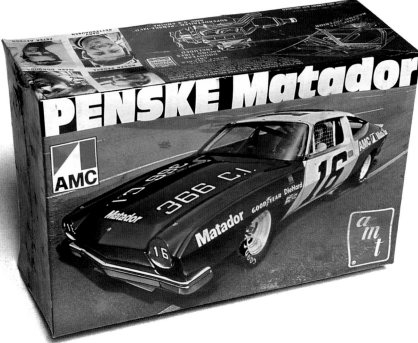

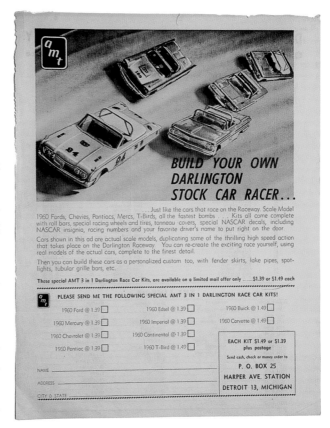

department store over the years. What kid hasn't attempted to assemble a model kit at least once?

Indianapolis cars, sports cars, street rods, and dragsters were among the most popular kits during the 1960s. Surprisingly, other than a few non-specific stock car kits, there were virtually no NASCAR kits manufactured until 1971, when the MPC Authentic NASCAR Series was introduced. It included many of the cars driven by NASCAR's top drivers—Richard Petty, Buddy Baker, David Pearson, Donnie Allison, Bobby Isaac, and Dick Brooks, to name a few. These $^1/_{24}$-scale model kits were quite realistic, packed in attractive boxes, and included the proper decals. The MPC kits are considered the pioneer plastic model kits for the NASCAR hobby and are quite valuable, especially if unassembled and sealed in their original boxes.

MPC expanded its first effort with the MPC NASCAR Exclusive License Series, which included kits for Cale Yarborough and Coo Coo Marlin, plus

two large-scale ($^1/_{16}$) kits for Petty and Baker. A few other stock car kits were issued by MPC during the 1970s, but the company concentrated mainly on passenger cars and other models.

AMT produced a line of NASCAR model kits in the mid-1970s; among them were Lennie Pond's Malibu, Benny Parsons' Chevrolet, and a Penske Matador driven by Bobby Allison. Johan produced two Petty Superbird models in the early 1970s, as well as a retrospective issue of Petty's 1964 Plymouth (which has since been reissued).

After a brief lull, there was a flurry of new kits in the mid-1980s as the demand for NASCAR

Because they were usually issued in much smaller quantities, large-scale NASCAR models are more difficult to find. This $^1/_{16}$th-scale model depicts Cale Yarborough's 1985 Ford Thunderbird, fielded by Harry Ranier Racing.

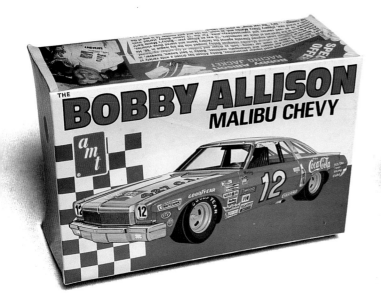

A Bobby Allison Chevy Malibu AMT $^1/_{24}$-scale model kit from the early 1970s. Like the early MPC NASCAR kits, this is a tough one to find. Allison won ten races, held twelve pole positions, and finished in the top ten in twenty-seven out of thirty-one starts in 1972, but he still finished second to Richard Petty in the point standings.

This Petty Plymouth Superbird model produced by Jo-Han in the early 1970s is scarce and in great demand by model collectors. The colorful artwork on the box contributes to its popularity.

models soared. Both Monogram and AMT issued a large number of kits highlighting NASCAR's new superstars like Bill Elliott, Dale Earnhardt, Terry Labonte, Rusty Wallace, and Darrell Waltrip. These early Monogram plastic kits are also very popular among NASCAR collectors. One of the rarest Monogram kits is for the two-car Budweiser team of Neil Bonnett and Darrell Waltrip. There have also been models of NASCAR transporters.

Monogram and AMT/ERTL have continued to be prolific makers of plastic models through the 1990s. These companies have added haulers, multi-car teams, and $^1/_{32}$-scale snap kits to their product lines. In the early 1980s, ERTL produced two metal kits featuring Richard Petty and Darrell Waltrip, which are now quite scarce. A Davey Allison $^1/_{32}$ kit had a special "Winner of the 1992 Daytona 500" sticker affixed to its box, making it more rare than other issues.

Another popular form of modeling is the high-quality $^1/_{43}$-scale models, most of which are resin or white metal kits produced in Europe. These models are very detailed and accurate, un-

A Coo Coo Marlin Chevrolet MPC model kit from the early 1970s. Part of the Authentic NASCAR Series, it is one of the few models that features a driver who never won a race. Marlin started 165 races in his career, finishing in the top ten fifty-one times, but never recorded a victory. He won a Daytona 500 qualifying race, but it was not a regular points race.

Monogram began producing plastic model kits in the early 1980s. While Dale Earnhardt's most successful seasons have been aboard the Goodwrench Chevrolet, he also ran a Ford Thunderbird in 1983 for Bud Moore. Ricky Rudd took over this ride in 1984 when Earnhardt moved over to Richard Childress Racing.

like the mass-produced diecast models imported from China and Taiwan. With the exception of Vitesse and a few other companies, $^1/_{43}$-scale kits do not have special packaging, so they are worth more assembled. However, most plastic kits are far more valuable when left in the box. Most $^1/_{43}$ kits are produced in very limited numbers and are difficult to find. Many NASCAR collectors are unaware they even exist since they are primarily available from mail-order companies specializing in European road racing models.

While plastic model manufacturers continue to produce new kits at a steady rate, there has been a dramatic shift among collectors toward diecast metal cars, which are already assembled and usually sturdier than delicate plastic models.

The art of building plastic model kits may be slowly fading away, but the kits remain a very popular collectible. Nevertheless, diecast cars are the wave of the future in NASCAR collecting.

Other Collectible Stock Cars in Miniature

During the 1960s, when slot car racing became the rage across America, several stock cars sets were produced. While most had standardized track layouts and fictional cars, some very collectible slot car racing sets were produced featuring NASCAR cars and drivers. In the early 1970s, Richard Petty and Bobby Allison were the first drivers to be depicted on the packaging of stock car racing sets. Later, Bill Elliott was pictured on a slot car set. It is difficult to find these sets in complete condition.

A relatively new segment of the collectible toys hobby is radio-controlled race cars. Several cars featuring leading NASCAR Winston Cup teams have been produced, most in large quantities. These tend to be collectible only if in the original packaging.

Liquor decanters have been produced portraying a variety of cars, but only a few have been of NASCAR stock cars.

Above left: An Ernie Irvan radio-controlled Kodak Winston Cup car, one of several different NASCAR radio-controlled cars issued in the late 1980s. Irvan won the 1991 Daytona 500 driving the McClure Racing Kodak Chevrolet.

Above: Radio-controlled toys that portray actual Winston Cup cars are very popular among NASCAR collectors. When still in its original packaging, this Dale Earnhardt Wrangler Monte Carlo, depicting the 1986 Winston Cup championship car, is quite valuable.

Liquor decanter showing the Bud Moore–owned Norris Thunderbird that Bobby Allison drove during the late 1970s. Allison won the 1978 Daytona 500 in this car and finished second in the Winston Cup standings behind Cale Yarborough.

KESBORO 1962

DAVID PEARSON

OTTON'S RIDE

BIG TRACK CHAMP

CHAPTER 6

Cards, Decals & Patches

Since the first baseball cards were packaged with cigarettes back in the 1880s, sports cards have been a mainstay of collectibles. The first auto racing card sets appeared around 1910, but it wasn't until the late 1980s that major card sets were produced exclusively for stock car racing.

The introduction of the first major NASCAR card set by Maxx in 1988 ignited an explosion in all types of NASCAR collectibles, creating a multimillion dollar industry.

Collector Cards

From an aesthetic standpoint, the first Maxx set was considered mediocre at best; however, it did not take long for other manufacturers to join the racing card fray. Soon the quality and quantity of sets grew by leaps and bounds. At the same time, several special promotional sets, regional issues, and other card promotions flooded the market.

By the early 1990s, cards sets were being produced by Action Packed, Pro Set, Traks, Finish Line, Press Pass, Wheels and others. Premium card sets, subsets, prototypes, metal cards, contest cards, and other gimmicks were used to attract collectors and create a perceived value to a hobby which was quickly becoming over-saturated.

Then the inevitable happened. Less than seven years after the introduction of cards to the NASCAR collecting hobby, the market is shrinking

Above: A Traks Richard Petty/STP Twentieth Anniversary pack. This set, featuring 50 cards, was issued in 1991 and is fairly common.

Opposite: The Masters of Racing set issued by T.G. Racing in 1989 was one of the first major card sets to feature famous stock car racing drivers from the past. Many of the photographs used to produce this set came from the archives of Racing Pictorial *magazine.*

The 1988 Maxx cards were the first major card set to feature NASCAR drivers. It ignited interest in all forms of racing collectibles, making NASCAR card collecting one of the fastest-growing segments of the sports collectibles industry. This set consists of 100 cards and includes drivers, tracks, and action shots.

as many manufacturers go out of business or scale back on production. In addition to the over-supply of cards, the market has been taken over in part by the growing popularity of diecast cars. The appeal of diecast cars, both visually and from the standpoint of variety, has caught the fancy of NASCAR fans.

Collector cards will no doubt always play a key part in the racing collectibles hobby. There are many attractive sets and some have appreciated in value during the few short years they have been on the market. And, like other sports, cards featuring superstars, such as Earnhardt, Elliott, Gordon, Petty, and Wallace are likely to be more in demand in future years.

The first two Maxx sets remain among the most desirable for NASCAR collectors. However, some little-known cards sets are sought by collectors. For example, the 1972 STP promotional series features ten NASCAR stars and is very difficult to find.

Above: Phone cards are a small segment of the card industry but their popularity is on the rise. These cards, issued by Finish Line, are made of heavy plastic and sold in various increments of telephone minutes. The most expensive cards are less common.

Right: The 1989 Maxx card set grew to 220 different cards and the graphics improved significantly. Its limited distribution compared to the years that followed make this a very popular set for collectors. Capitalizing on a renewed interest in NASCAR history, this set also includes many famous drivers from the past.

RUSTY WALLACE

1989 WINSTON CUP CHAMPION

1987 V

RICHARD PETTY

1971 WINSTON CUP CHAMPION

1973

Post Cards

One of the oldest specialties of the racing card hobby are post cards. Since the 1950s, stock car racing post cards have been issued by various publications, sponsors, teams, and tracks. Like many other types of racing memorabilia, the Indy 500 was the originator of post cards and special post card sets. Hundreds of different post cards have been printed since 1909 portraying the Indianapolis Motor Speedway.

Above: A Tim Richmond Old Milwaukee promotional card from the early 1980s. Richmond first made his mark in the Indianapolis 500, winning Rookie of the Year in 1980. He joined the Winston Cup circuit on a full-time basis in 1981.

Left: A Twentieth Anniversary Winston Cup Champions card set depicting each car that won the NASCAR title since 1973, when Winston began sponsoring the series. The sets were part of a promotional offer with Winston cigarettes.

DAYTONA INTERNATIONAL SPEEDWAY

Stock car racing post cards became quite popular in the 1960s and 1970s, followed in the early 1980s by a tremendous boom of promotional cards that were roughly the same size as post cards, but not meant for mailing. Every year, dozens of promotional cards are issued by major NASCAR teams and sponsors. They are usually handed out free at races and other special events. Some of these have become quite collectible over the years, depending on their level of production.

Patches, Decals, and Buttons

Patches, decals, and buttons have been a way for fans to wear their allegiance to products, teams, drivers, and manufactures involved with racing. Often colorful and designed in a variety of shapes and sizes, these items have been popular among collectors for many years.

Photographs of drivers during the 1950s and 1960s reveal very few patches on their uniforms.

DAYTONA INTERNATIONAL SPEEDWAY

*Like father, like son. These post cards, issued by Racing
Pictorial magazine in the early 1960s, show father-son
race car drivers. On the left is Richard and Lee Petty, who
combined for 354 NASCAR Grand National wins. On*

 MELL-GEAR Co. • 3506 Scheele Drive, •Jackson, MI 49204

Two promotional cards from the Melling Tool Team in the early 1980s. Drivers for the team were established star Benny Parsons, and a little-known driver from Dawsonville, Georgia, named Bill Elliott. Note the small Daytona International Speedway control tower in the background, which has now been replaced by the Winston Tower.

Melling Tool Co. • 2620 Saradan Drive, • Jackson, MI 49204

A variety of colorful team and sponsor stickers have been handed out at NASCAR races over the years. Literally thousands of decals and stickers have been produced. While most are very common, they make a nice display.

As major companies began to sponsor stock car racing teams, more and more patches appeared. By the same token, stock cars are now covered with sponsor decals, unlike the early years of racing in which cars look rather plain by today's standards.

Patches became very popular among race fans in the 1960s. Virtually every racing event, track, and sponsor produced souvenir cloth patches. Many race fans put them on their jackets and shirts, and most of them were eventually discarded. Cloth patches vary in size, quality, and design. Racing decals (called stickers by today's race fans) date back to the 1930s. Virtually all the early decals were water soluble (soak-ons) and usually ended up affixed on the side of cars. The use of decals proliferated in the late 1950s and 1960s. Equipment manufacturers were anxious to get their names on race cars, thus a huge variety of product decals were distributed.

Peel-off stickers and pressure-sensitive decals became popular in the late 1960s. Literally thousands of different stickers have been printed since the 1970s depicting a huge variety of cars, drivers, and products. Today, computer-cut tape decals are becoming the predominant method of decal production.

Many older decals tend to yellow or crack due to age. Finding an old decal in perfect condition

Stock car racing stickers and decals are inexpensive collectibles that virtually any race fan can afford.

An early 1960s cloth patch from the Southern 500 showing the Confederate flag logo and the Atlanta International Raceway.

A track patch from Darlington in the early 1960s.

Collector pins are a fast-growing segment of the stock car racing souvenir market. Shown at far left is a pin issued by Kodak to commemorate Ernie Irvan's Daytona 500 victory aboard the Kodak Chevrolet. Dale Jarrett's first Daytona 500 win in 1993 is highlighted on the pin shown left. Pins are usually mass-produced and not generally favored by serious memorabilia collectors.

is very difficult. Generally speaking, decals and patches that are dated for a specific event, commemorate an anniversary, or are associated with a specific race team in a given year are more valuable than general-sponsorship logo patches. Dated technical inspection decals issued by NASCAR for competition cars are very rare, although these and many other decals are now being reproduced.

Thanks to political campaigns, buttons have been around for well over a hundred years. A very popular collectible, pin-back racing buttons (both celluloid and tin) have been used for many years.

Since the early 1960s, buttons have been issued by race tracks for different types of credentials, while souvenir dealers have sold buttons featuring leading NASCAR drivers and cars for many years.

Collector pins are a more recent phenomenon. Often measuring less than an inch across, these small pins (usually with screw or snap posts) have been produced by the millions. NASCAR fans often wear their button collections on their favorite racing hat. As with other stock car racing memorabilia, dated buttons and pins are the most collectible.

Daytona International Speedway

This post card shows the inaugural Dayona 500 held in 1959.

NASCAR celebrated its twenty-fifth year in 1973 by incorporating this Silver Anniversary design into its existing logo. All NASCAR publications that year featured this logo.

A Daytona pennant from the early 1960s.

CHAPTER 7

Miscellaneous Collectibles

Aside from the more traditional categories of collecting—such as programs, models, diecast cars, and trading cards—many other unique items produced over the past five decades have become valued collectibles.

Record Albums

While vinyl record albums may be a thing of the past, there have been several collectible albums produced on stock car racing.

Richard Petty has been the subject of two record albums, *Meet Richard Petty* and *I've Never Been Scared in a Race Car*, both of which are popular among collectors, although not particularly rare. Albums featuring the Rebel 300, Firecracker 400,

Daytona 500, and World 600 were also produced in the 1960s. As with any type of record album, the condition of the jacket is very important; those still factory-sealed are the most desirable from a collecting standpoint.

Event Posters

Unlike sports car, Indy car, and Formula One racing—where poster art has become a tradition—very few NASCAR tracks still produce

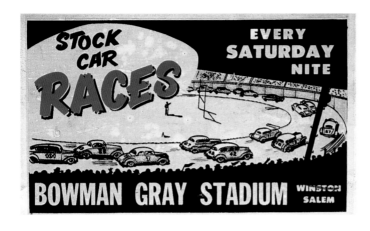

Left: Advertising decal from Bowman-Gray Stadium in Winston-Salem, North Carolina, during the 1950s. This track was built in 1947 and hosted NASCAR Grand National races from 1958 to 1971.

Opposite: A Dale Earnhardt collectible plate. Most manufacturers of such items will individually number each plate and advertise the total number produced.

They treat their dames - and their cars the same-ROUGH!

...The guys who drive faster, love harder and swing higher than anyone else on earth!

AMERICAN INTERNATIONAL presents

FIREBALL 500

IN PANAVISION® and COLOR

STARRING
FRANKIE AVALON · ANNETTE FUNICELLO · FABIAN · CHILL WILLS
HARVEY LEMBECK · JULIE PARRISH written by WILLIAM ASHER and LEO TOWNSEND

posters. From the 1950s through the late 1970s, many tracks distributed posters that have now become very collectible, especially those from the very early years of stock car racing. The Globe poster company printed many of the posters back in the 1950s, and although they are somewhat general, they are also popular among collectors because they make attractive displays.

Commemorative posters and sponsor-issued posters (such as the Busch Clash and Winston Select posters) are also popular among some race fans, though dated event posters are the most valued by collectors.

Display Items

Racing items not originally intended to be collectible often turn out to be the rarest and most desirable forms of racing memorabilia. Such has proven to be the case with display items. This rather broad category encompasses just about any item produced as a display for retail products, including banners, cardboard standups, and other point-of-sale items.

Display items are perhaps one of the most unusual segments of the hobby. These items are produced in relatively small quantities and, until a few years ago, seldom ended up in the hands of collectors.

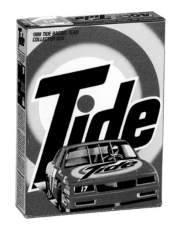

Above: In 1985, Bill Elliott won the Winston Million at Darlington by also winning at Daytona and Talladega during the same season. In victory lane, hundreds of these "million-dollar bills" were handed out with a picture of Bill Elliott (note his name is spelled wrong). These are now quite rare. A special souvenir cup (far right) from that same event is more common.

Opposite (far left): Movie posters about stock car racing are a great addition to any collection. This poster is from a movie titled "Fireball 500" starring Frankie Avalon, Annette Funicello, and Fabian.

Opposite (left): This Tide box from 1988 is a landmark item for racing collectors. Tide was one of the first major products not related to autos, beer, or cigarettes to become affiliated with stock car racing on a national scale. This opened a floodgate for other consumer products—from panty hose to deodorant—and confirmed corporate America's acknowledgment of NASCAR as a major league sport. The box shows Darrell Waltrip's Tide Chevrolet, winner of the 1987 Daytona 500.

This Bill Elliott Barbecue Sauce is an example of the hundreds of consumer products that feature NASCAR stars. The sauce came out in 1992.

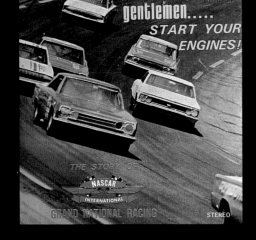

Above and opposite: Several record albums featuring NASCAR racing have been produced. While most of them are not particularly rare, they are fun to listen to (but worth more to collectors if still sealed).

Left: Store display items such as this Richard Petty headache powders display are in great demand by NASCAR collectors. Not originally intended to be collectibles, many prior to 1990 are quite scarce since most are discarded before they reach the hands of collectors.

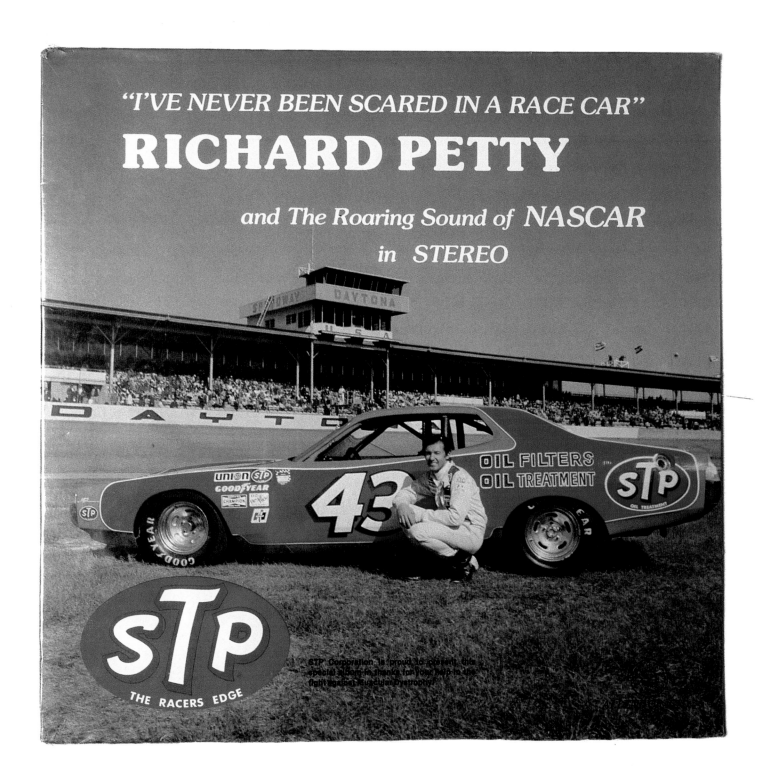

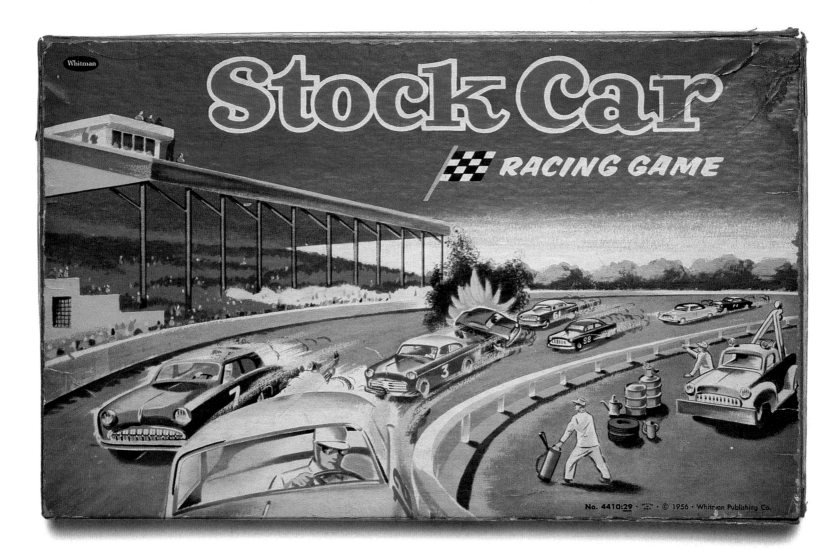

Several board games featuring stock car racing have been produced since the 1950s. "The Stock Car Racing Game" was issued by Whitman Game Company in 1956. "The 300 Mile Race" game came out in the early 1960s. Both games are generalized and do not depict actual NASCAR tracks or drivers.

This rather nondescript piece of paper contains a very historic signature—Johnny Mantz, winner of the first Southern 500 in 1950. It was his only NASCAR win. Mantz was killed in a traffic accident in 1972.

Consumer products with a NASCAR racing collectible theme have been increasingly popular in recent years. Soft drinks, beer cans and bottles, cereal boxes, laundry detergent, and auto parts are just a few of the dozens of products which feature NASCAR drivers, cars, and tracks.

Product displays have become very elaborate and attractive. Lighted signs and full-color, life-size driver photographs are two of the many different types of store displays seen in supermarkets and department stores. It is very difficult to find these kinds of items dating from before 1980, since NASCAR had yet to reach its nationwide popularity and few drivers had attained the name recognition to warrant such displays. One exception is a battery additive from the late 1950s which featured Lee Petty on packaging and store displays.

Board Games

Several board games have been produced on stock car racing. Most of them depict fictional tracks and drivers. Buck Baker was one of the first NASCAR stars to have a board game produced. These games are most valuable when the box art is attractive and the game is still complete and in excellent condition.

Autographs

Autograph collecting has been a major part of baseball and other sports collecting hobbies for several years. NASCAR driver autographs are also becoming a popular collectible. Signatures of legendary drivers who have passed on are the most valuable, such as Fireball Roberts, Joe Weatherly, and Curtis Turner. Collectors need to be very careful when buying such signatures, however, because this part of the hobby has been plagued by forgeries. For historical reasons, signatures on event programs, letters, and original photographs are usually the most valuable.

It is always best to obtain your autographs in person. Fortunately, NASCAR drivers are very receptive to giving autographs.

Artwork

Artwork is a relatively new form of collectible among NASCAR fans. While road racing artwork has been popular for many years, only recently has NASCAR art gained a wide following. Well-known artists such as Garry Hill, Buz McKim, Sam Bass, and Simon Ward have produced high-quality, thoroughly researched artwork, often concentrating on historic aspects of the sport.

Of course, art is subjective. Don't buy something just because you know the name of the artist. Racing art should be purchased because you like it.

NASCAR

FEATURE WINNER

Opposite and left: NASCAR official decals issued for application on race cars are very hard to find. They usually indicated the car had passed technical inspection. Most decals from the 1950s and 1960s are dated.

Left: This decal issued by Wynn's Friction Proofing in 1961 is very rare. It shows the three most recent NASCAR Grand National Champions: Ned Jarrett (note his name is spelled wrong), Rex White, and Lee Petty.

Below: Wynn's decal shows the top three finishers in the 1953 Southern 500. Buck Baker, Fonty Flock, and Curtis Turner, all of whom, of course, used Wynn's Friction Proofing in their cars. Other than automotive-related products, NASCAR drivers were seldom used for product endorsements during the 1950s since the sport had yet to become popular on a national scale.

Other NASCAR-produced Items

During the first fifty years of NASCAR, the sanctioning organization produced many items for its membership which have been very collectible. NASCAR competition decals are popular among both memorabilia collectors and those who specialize in the restoration of old NASCAR cars, although these water-based decals are very rare. These decals, usually dated, were affixed to competition cars and few survive unused.

NASCAR event entry forms are another unusual collectible that has become popular among

A Miller Brewing Company retail display sign that depicts the Daytona 500 in the early 1970s. Such items were not offered to the public and were generally produced in small quantities.

serious stock car racing collectors. These are usually four-page brochures that list prize money and other information teams needed before entering an event. Entry forms from the Southern 500 and Daytona 500 are quite rare.

Many race fans today are unaware that NASCAR sanctioned Indy car, sports car, midget car, and drag racing events. In the early 1950s, the NASCAR Speedway Division was formed. This was for Indy cars with engines from American cars. While the events were a success from a competition standpoint, race fans in the South did not attend in the same numbers as the Grand National events and the Speedway Division was dissolved after only two years.

In the 1960s, NASCAR formed a drag racing division. Rule books and other drag racing items from NASCAR are very rare. NASCAR also sanctioned sports car events in the late 1950s and midget racing events from the late 1950s through the 1960s. Very few items exist regarding this aspect of NASCAR history.

Many NASCAR items can be identified by the style of the logo used. Nineteen seventy-eight marked the introduction of the NASCAR "color bar" logo, which is still in use today. It replaced the "facing streamline cars" design which had been used since the inception of NASCAR with only minor modifications.

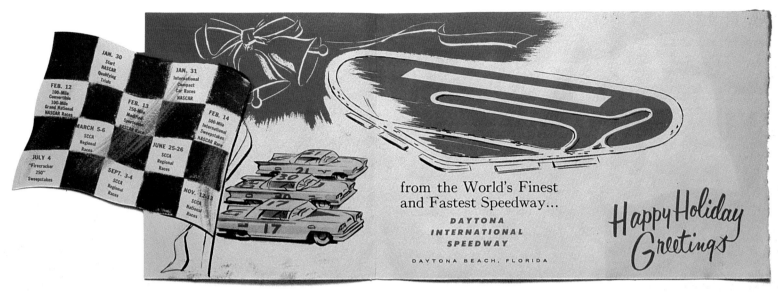

from the World's Finest
and Fastest Speedway...

**DAYTONA
INTERNATIONAL
SPEEDWAY**

DAYTONA BEACH, FLORIDA

Happy Holiday Greetings

Above: A Daytona International Speedway Christmas card from 1960. Its artwork and design make it an attractive collectible. The schedule for the upcoming season is shown in the checkered flag.

Left: Artwork depicting NASCAR racing is becoming very popular among race fans and serious collectors. This Garry Hill print represents one of the finest historic scenes of racing on Daytona Beach.

Terminology has also changed in NASCAR over the years. The term "Strictly Stock" was used primarily during the 1948–1954 era, while the premier series was known as "Grand National" up to 1983. In a confusing move that racing historians still find misleading, the Grand National name was reassigned to the supporting Sportsman series, and the premier series was renamed Winston Cup.

With NASCAR celebrating its fiftieth anniversary in 1998, increased awareness of NASCAR history will likely result in all types of memorabilia relating to the sanctioning body becoming more in demand.

Purolator Car 21
The winningest car in NASCAR history
1st. Daytona 500 Daytona Beach, F
1st. Miller High Life 500 Ontario
1st. Rebel 400 Darlington, S.C.
1st. Winston 500 Talladega, A
1st. Motor State 400 Irish H
1st. Firecracker 400 Daytn
1st. Yankee 400 Irish Hill
1st. Delaware 500 Do
2nd. Southern 500 Ta

clean
performance
clean
performance
clean
performance
clean
performance
clean
performance
change now!
oil
air
gasoline
filters
PUROLATOR

Bumper Stickers and License Plates

Bumper stickers have been around for as long as NASCAR, and there have been plenty produced over the years. Since most of the early ones ended up on chrome bumpers, these are difficult to find. NASCAR issued several versions of the "If You Want to Race, Join NASCAR" bumper

sticker during the 1950s and 1960s. Soon after, bumper stickers were issued representing the stars of NASCAR, especially Richard Petty. By the late 1970s, race sponsors recognized bumper stickers as an effective advertising tool, and hundreds of them featuring leading drivers have been produced since then.

Many tracks have issued souvenir license plates including Atlanta, Charlotte, Darlington, Daytona, and Talladega. Metal plates from the 1960s and 1970s are scarce and difficult to find in excellent condition. Most souvenir license plates are now plastic.

Apparel

Although racing shirts, jackets, and hats are the biggest segment of the racing souvenir industry, they are seldom placed in the same category as memorabilia. Apparel is mass-produced and can be reissued easily by the manufacturer, detracting from its collectibility.

There are some categories of apparel that are worth collecting, however. Team apparel used by pit crews and others on major NASCAR teams

Entry form for the first Southern 500 in 1950.
Note that the race was originally to be sanctioned
by the CSRA, but NASCAR took over organiza-
tion of the event.

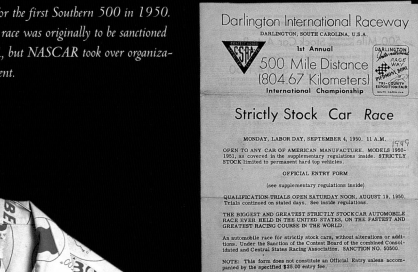

This hard-to-find shirt was sold by
Darlington Raceway during the 1960s.

Even though most collectors
consider hats to be souvenirs and
therefore not collectible, this one
from the last NASCAR Winston
Cup race at North Wilkesboro will
likely be worth saving.

A souvenir Daytona 500 metal license plate from the early 1960s. Today, most souvenir plates are made of plastic.

Left: A metal pin-back button from the World 600 at Charlotte during the mid-1960s. Below is a bumper sticker from the World 600 during the 1960s. The race is now known as the Coca-Cola 600.

"WORLD
MAY 2
CHARLOTTE MO

A Richard Petty bumper sticker from the early 1970s. "King Richard" dominated Winston Cup competition during this period and became stock car racing's first nationally recognized superstar.

RICHARD PETTY

King Of NASCAR

RICHARD PETTY RACING TEAM FAN CLUB
43

600"

TOR SPEEDWAY

Hats, T-shirts, and jackets have been a mainstay of race fans for decades. Since they can easily be reissued, these souvenirs generally have no collecting value. Dated items are the most popular, such as this 1989 Daytona 500 hat. High-quality wearables, such as this Bill Elliott leather jacket, will probably retain their value.

has become very popular among collectors. Driver helmets and uniforms are the most valued in this category, often bringing fairly high prices.

Keep in mind that manufacturers often make uniforms which are never actually worn by the driver, so it is difficult to determine the authenticity. Helmets are also difficult to verify, since they can be painted to match an original. When possible, try to obtain a letter from the driver stating they actually wore the uniform or helmet in a race.

There are some special types of souvenir apparel now desired by collectors, such as the famous Darlington shirts from the early 1960s and NASCAR officials' jackets from the 1950s and 1960s.

Car Parts

Perhaps the ultimate example of stock car racing memorabilia is a piece of an actual stock car. Hoods, fenders, doors, bumpers, and other sheet metal that clearly indicates what car they are from are very popular among collectors and make excellent display items. In addition, pit boards, fueling cans, and other race team items are also appealing, particularly if they are from the 1950s and 1960s.

Tires and mechanical car parts are far less desirable since they *could* be from any car. Some companies have marketed these car parts, but they lack the appeal of sheet metal that has sponsor decals and car numbers which readily identify the car.

At one time, car parts were discarded by teams and could simply be taken for the asking. Now these items are often held for auctions or special sales.

*UNOCAL's Bill Brodrick reviews a clothesline of collectible
driver's uniforms at Darlington in 1990. From front to back,
they belong to Geoff Bodine, Mark Martin, Dale Earnhardt,
Rusty Wallace, and Bill Elliott. Brodrick is best known to fans
as the man who greeted Winston Cup winners in victory lane
and coordinated the changing of sponsors' hats.*

LOCKHART MEMORIAL

STOCK CAR

RACE

15 % NET TO COMMUNITY FUND

SUNDAY

Collecting Resources

Books

Forty Years of Stock Car Racing

By Greg Fielden

A multi-volume set that gives a summary of every NASCAR Grand National/Winston Cup event ever held, including finishing results and yearly points standings. An invaluable reference for the serious collector.

Gallery of Legends

Published by International Speedway Corp. Publications

P.O. Box 2801

Daytona Beach, FL 32120

Pictorial History of Racing at Daytona Beach from 1903 to present.

Collecting Publications

Beckett Racing Monthly

Beckett Publications, Inc.

15850 Dallas Parkway

Dallas, TX 75248

A good source for information and values on more recent collectibles, especially cards and diecast.

RPM

Tuff Stuff Publications, Inc.

1934 E. Parham Road

Richmond, VA 23228

A monthly magazine covering diecast and cars (formerly known as *Collector's World of Racing*).

Mobilia

P.O Box 575

Middlebury, VT 05753

Monthly magazine devoted to all types of automotive collectibles, with emphasis on older items.

Opposite: A poster from the Lockhart Memorial Stock Car Race at Daytona Beach in 1941. The race was named in honor of 1926 Indy winner Frank Lockhart, who was killed attempting to break the land speed record on Daytona Beach. A grandstand at Daytona International Speedway is named after Lockhart.

Racing Publications

Stock Car Racing
General Media Automotive Group
65 Parker Street, #2
Newburyport, MA 01950

National Speed Sport News
P.O. Box 1210
Harrisburg, NC 28075

NASCAR Winston Cup Scene
Street & Smith's Sports Group
128 South Tryon Street, Suite 2275
Charlotte, NC 28202

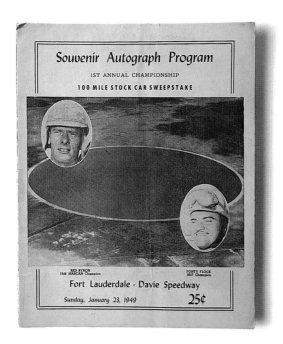

Shows

Throughout the year, there are hundreds of local shows devoted primarily to new collectibles such as diecast toys and collectibles. For serious collectors, the biggest show of the year is the National Auto Racing Memorabilia Expo held at the Indiana Convention Center the Friday and Saturday before the Indianapolis 500. For twenty years, this has been *the* show for collectors of all types of auto racing memorabilia.

For those interested in older NASCAR memorabilia, a show devoted to stock car racing memorabilia at least ten years old is held annually in Daytona Beach the Thursday and Friday prior to the Daytona 500. For more information on these shows write Auto Racing Memories, P.O. Box 12226, St. Petersburg, Florida 33733.

Acknowledgments

Special Thanks to Marty Little for allowing items in his collection to be photographed. We are also grateful for information provided by Jim Wolffbrandt, Dick Greene, and Bill Chubbuck.

This program is from a 1949 NASCAR event held at the Fort Lauderdale-Davie Speedway, which was actually an airport near Fort Lauderdale. (It is now the site of a college.) Featured on the cover are NASCAR's first two champions, Red Byron and Fonty Flock. NASCAR programs dating prior to 1950 are rare.

About the Author

Ken Breslauer is America's leading authority on auto racing memorabilia. A collector for over twenty-five years, he owns one of the most diverse collections of racing artifacts known to exist, featuring memorabilia from NASCAR, the Indianapolis 500, and the 12 Hours of Sebring. The promoter of the annual National Auto Racing Memorabilia Expo in Indianapolis, Ken is also the track historian for Sebring International Raceway.

Fonty Flock (#500B) aboard his Dodge on the way to a tenth place finish in the 1956 Daytona Beach Grand National race. Fonty's brother Tim won the race driving a Chevy, followed by Bill Myers in a Mercury. Also shown is the Chevrolet of Harvey Henderson (#19)

A former sports writer, he is the author of *Sebring, The Official History of America's Great Sports Car Race*, which was chosen 1996 Book of the Year by the American Auto Racing Writers and Broadcasters Association. He resides in St. Petersburg, Florida.

FUTURE HOME
DAYTONA
INTERNATIONAL SPEEDWAY

OPENING
FEB.
1959

PURE Gasoline Official Fuel

This sign, erected in 1957 on property along U.S. 92 west of Daytona Beach, marked the proposed location for Daytona International Speedway. Construction began late that year and the speedway was finished in January 1959, in time for the inaugural Speed Week.